# TOP SCORE

## WORKBOOK 2

HELEN HALLIWELL

OXFORD

UNIVERSITY PRESS

# OXFORD
UNIVERSITY PRESS

Great Clarendon Street, Oxford OX2 6DP

Oxford University Press is a department of the University of Oxford.
It furthers the University's objective of excellence in research, scholarship,
and education by publishing worldwide in

Oxford  New York

Auckland  Cape Town  Dar es Salaam  Hong Kong  Karachi
Kuala Lumpur  Madrid  Melbourne  Mexico City  Nairobi
New Delhi  Shanghai  Taipei  Toronto

With offices in

Argentina  Austria  Brazil  Chile  Czech Republic  France  Greece
Guatemala  Hungary  Italy  Japan  Poland  Portugal  Singapore
South Korea  Switzerland  Thailand  Turkey  Ukraine  Vietnam

**Photocopying**

ISBN-13: 978 0 19 412905 3

Printed in China

ACKNOWLEDGEMENTS

The author would like to thank everyone who has helped in the creation of
this book, especially James Styring and the staff of Oxford University Press.

*The publishers would like to thank the following for their kind permission to reproduce
photographs and other copyright material*: Action Plus p17 (Selima Sfar/Glyn Kirk);
Alamy pp 3 (Blend Images/newsreader), 4 (Detail Nottingham/petition, Libby
Welch/bottle bank, Steve Allen/airmail envelope), 5 (girl running/FogStock), 6
(girl playing basketball), 14 (Dynamic Graphics Group/ swimmer), 16 (Owen
Robson/skier, Lucidio Studios Inc/tennis player), 19 (floating village on lake,
Cambodia/Henry Westheim Photography ), 28 (Burj Al Arab), 31 (Martin
Cushey/marathon runners), 33 (Rick Dekker/hockey), 41 (Pixonnet.com/ice
hotel, Ian Dagnall/Guadix cave house), 42 (Picture Partners/ teenage girls), 48
(Men playing hockey/Cut and Deal Ltd), 50 (Pixonnet.com/ice hotel), 51 (S.T.
Yiap/Sydney Harbour Bridge), 55 (I.T. Stock Free/girl playing flute), 57 (James
Osmond/Borneo river), 58 (Steve Knott/quokka), 64 (Big Ben New Years Eve
fireworks London), 65 (Big Cheese Photo/rock band), 69 (Blickwinkel/bird), 70
(Mike Abrahams ), 72 (Christian Darkin/yeti); Corbis pp 3 (Reuters/quiz show,
Bob Marshak/Columbia Pictures/Bureau L.A. Collections/chef, Steve
Chen/sports, David Aubrey/tree frog), 4 (© Royalty Free/food packaging, Bisson
Bernard/protest, Charles O'Rear/factory), 15 (Tim de Waele/cyclists), 18 (Phil
Noble/Reuters/Rafael Benítez), 22 (Elizabeth Kreutz/New Sport/Franz
Ferdinand), 23 (Kieran Doherty/Kelly Clarkson), 27 (Brian Bailey/women
jogging), 35, 38 (Toru Hanal/Reuters/digital camera, © Royalty Free/speakers,
printer), 45 (Rolf Bruderer/interior), 61 (Michael Busselle/Asturias), 72
(Christopher Farina/TVs, Randy Faris/umbrellas, Sergei Chirikov/epa/Dennis
Tito); Getty pp 10 (Angela Capetta/teenage girl), 13 (David Beckham Academy),
26 (David Odonkor /Lars Baron), 27 (AFP/Harry Potter book cover); OUP pp 3
(men playing judo), 19 (river barge/Russ Merne), 38 (© OUP Royalty Free/cable,
keyboard, mouse, MP3 player, monitor), 66 (hands holding money/Ingram);
PunchStock p21 (Businesswoman using a computer/Blend); Rex pp 3 (Everett
Collection/cartoon), 7 (Goldwyn/Everett Collection/*Super Size Me*), 28 (Zaha
Hadid/Karl Schoendorfer), 28 (The Palm), 29 (Fogle and Cracknell), 41
(Poseidon Underwater Resort), 50 (Fogle and Cracknell, Sipa Press/Alain
Robert), 51 (James D. Morgan/Sydney Harbour Bridge guides), 63 (Ilpo
Musto/chewing gum noticeboard).

*Illustrations by*: Rui Ricardo/Folio London  pp 8, 12, 20, 26, 30, 36, 44, 47, 49,
64, 71.

# Getting started

## Vocabulary

### Personality adjectives and pastimes

**1** Complete the text with the words in the box.

> friendly  having  lazy  meeting  ~~shy~~  sociable

Some people think that I'm shy because I don't like (1) _____ parties. In fact, I love (2) _____ new people and I'm actually very (3) _____ and (4) _____. However, I prefer going to parties at other people's houses because I'm (5) _____!

### Travel and prepositions of movement

**2** Complete the puzzle. What is the mystery travel noun?

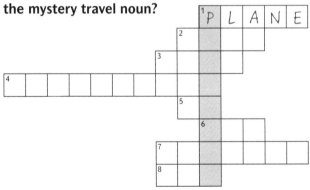

The mystery travel noun is _____.

1 You catch a _____ at an airport.
2 We have to wait for the flight at _____ 32.
3 You show your ticket at the check-in _____.
4 The flight _____ were really friendly.
5 Go _____ the escalator to the first floor.
6 Some people don't like taking _____.
7 Go _____ those doors to Terminal 1.
8 When can we _____ on the plane?

### Television and extreme adjectives

**3** Complete the types of programme with the correct letters. Then match 1–6 with a–f.

1 [b] t h e  n e w s
2 [ ] c _ o _ e _ y  _ r _ g _ a _ m _
3 [ ] d _ c _ m _ n _ a _ y
4 [ ] q _ i _  s _ o _
5 [ ] s _ o _ t _  p _ o _ r _ m _ e
6 [ ] c _ r _ o _ n

**4** Match the extreme adjectives 1–6 with the definitions a–e. Use one definition twice.

1 [c] brilliant
2 [ ] astonishing
3 [ ] hilarious
4 [ ] terrifying
5 [ ] wonderful
6 [ ] fascinating

a really funny
b really interesting
c really good
d really incredible
e really frightening

# Town and country

**5** Choose the correct answer.

We can't see a film because there isn't a stadium / (cinema) here.

1 They make shoes in that **factory** / **station**.

2 Where's the **train** / **fire** station? I want to go to London.

3 That's the football **village** / **stadium**.

4 Let's walk through the **hill** / **woods**.

5 My shoes got wet in the **stream** / **station**.

6 My grandparents live in a **factory** / **cottage** in the country.

# Adjectives of emotion

**6** Complete the sentences with the words in the box.

afraid ~~anxious~~ grateful proud relaxed
tense upset

I hate flying. I always feel *anxious*.

1 Steve is on holiday, so he's _____.

2 Gill is so moody. The atmosphere is always _____ at her house.

3 Patrick is _____ of dogs.

4 My parents were very _____ when I passed my exams.

5 They were _____ for everyone's help.

6 Ella was _____ when she heard the bad news.

# *go, make, do* and *have*

**7** Complete the sentences with *go, make, do* or *have*.

They *have* a shower every morning.

1 Our school didn't _____ a picnic last year.

2 We often _____ mistakes in our homework.

3 Did you _____ the washing up?

4 Shall we _____ on foot? There isn't a bus.

5 'I'm hungry!' 'OK, I'll _____ dinner.'

6 I _____ my homework in my bedroom.

# Environment

**8** Label the photographs.

packaging      1 f_____

2 d_____      3 p_____

4 l_____      5 b_____ b_____

# School

**9** Complete the crossword.

|  ¹T |   |  ²  |   |  ³  |   |  ⁴  |   |
|-----|---|-----|---|-----|---|-----|---|
|  E  |   |     |   |     |   |     |   |
| ⁵X  |   |     |   |     |   |     |   |
|  T  |   |     |   |     |   |     |   |
|  B  |   |     |   |     |   |     |   |
|  O  |   |     |   |     |   |     |   |
|  O  |   |     |   |     |   |     |   |
|  K  |   |     |   |     |   |     |   |

**Down (↓)**

1 You don't write in your _____.

2 You carry your things to school in a _____.

3 You have different _____ during the school day.

4 History, geography and maths are school _____.

**Across (→)**

2 The _____ tell you what you can and can't do at school.

5 You write in an _____ _____ at school.

# Grammar

## Present simple or present continuous?

**1** Read the text. Underline nine verbs in the present simple and two verbs in the present continuous.

Fourteen-year-old schoolgirl, Emily Hunt, lives with her family in Chatham, Kent. She goes to Chatham Girls' School – she isn't wearing her school uniform in the photo, but she usually wears it to school! Three times a week, Emily doesn't do any homework after school because she trains for two hours at her local running club. She is a brilliant runner. In fact, Emily is training to participate in the 2012 Olympic Games. Training so frequently isn't easy, but Emily is always enthusiastic and she often imagines winning an Olympic gold medal. Good luck, Emily!

**2** Write the questions.

how old / be / Emily ?
How old is Emily?

1 where / Emily and her family / live?
_____

2 boys / go / to Emily's school?
_____

3 what / students at her school / wear?
_____

4 how often / Emily / run / after school?
_____

5 how long / be / the training sessions / at the running club?
_____
_____

6 what / Emily / want / to do in the future?
_____
_____

7 what / Emily / do / in the photo?
_____
_____

8 Emily / wear / a uniform in the photo?
_____
_____

**3** Read the text in exercise 1 again and answer the questions in exercise 2.

Emily is fourteen years old.

1 _____
_____

2 _____
_____

3 _____
_____

4 _____
_____

5 _____
_____

6 _____
_____

7 _____
_____

8 _____
_____

## Adverbs of frequency

**4** Write sentences about you and your family. Use the present simple and the adverbs in the box.

| always usually often sometimes never |
| --- |

watch / reality shows
We sometimes watch reality shows.

1 listen / to the news on the radio
_____
_____

2 go / to the cinema
_____

3 cycle / to school
_____

4 send / text messages to my friends
_____
_____

5 do / the washing up
_____

6 recycle / used paper
_____

# Comparatives and superlatives

**5** Write sentences. Use the present simple form of the verbs and the comparative form of the adjectives.

> Alex / not be / old / than Gina
> *Alex isn't older than Gina.*

1 Tom / get up / late / than me

_____

_____

2 those flight attendants / be / friendly / than the others

_____

_____

3 they / live / far / from school / than us

_____

_____

4 your book / look / interesting / than mine

_____

_____

5 be / this textbook / long / than yours / ?

_____

_____

6 James / work / hard / than Ben

_____

_____

**6** Complete the sentences with the comparative or superlative form of the adjectives.

> The weather is *warmer* (warm) than yesterday.

1 Brazil is _____ (large) country in South America.
2 Russia is _____ (big) than France.
3 This red bag is _____ (good) than the blue one.
4 Jane is _____ (short) girl in the class.
5 That's _____ (funny) joke I've ever heard!
6 My brother and sister are _____ (intelligent) than me.

**7** Correct the mistake in each sentence.

> Nadal is best tennis player in Spain.
> *Nadal is the best tennis player in Spain.*

1 Never we go to the cinema.

_____

2 Mark is sending me emails every day.

_____

3 Live you near the stadium?

_____

4 Eva is more taller than Laura.

_____

5 We watch cartoons at the moment.

_____

6 I'm not understanding this question.

_____

## Consolidation

**8** Choose the correct answer.

Paula

This (**is**) / is being my sister, Paula. We **(1)** goes / go to the same school, but we **(2)** always / never travel together. Paula enjoys walking, so she **(3)** is getting up / gets up early and **(4)** goes / is going to school on foot.

I **(5)** don't walk / 'm not walking because I'm **(6)** more lazier / lazier than her. Sometimes I cycle to school, but I **(7)** usually / always catch the bus.

Paula is sporty, too. She **(8)** plays / 's playing basketball on the school team. In fact, she **(9)** plays / 's playing in a match at the moment. She loves winning. She says that it's **(10)** best / the best feeling in the world!

# 1 | Lifestyles

## Reading

# You are what you eat

**A** Can you imagine eating nothing except fast food for a whole month? That is exactly what a film-maker in the USA decided to do. Morgan Spurlock ate a diet of McDonald's food three times a day for 30 days because he wanted to investigate the effects of fast food on his health.

**B** While he was doing the diet, he made a film of his experiences. Near the end of the diet, Spurlock became very ill because the fast food was having a terrible effect on his body. His doctors told him, 'Stop eating fast food – or you will die.' His film, *Super Size Me,* was a huge hit in 2004.

**C** In the same year, a journalist in the UK tried the same unhealthy lifestyle, but only for seven days and seven nights. Before starting, Tim Adams went to a special clinic. The doctors told him that he was fit and healthy. Afterwards, he went to a fast food restaurant to have lunch and to start the experiment.

**D** At the beginning, Adams felt cheerful and optimistic about everything. However, by day four, he was feeling miserable and his wife noticed that he was moodier than normal. On day seven, Adams went back to the clinic to see the doctors. The results were dramatic. After only a week, he was overweight and very unhealthy. 'You are what you eat,' said Adams, 'and I feel awful!'

**1** Read the text. Match paragraphs A–D with headings 1–5. (There is one heading you do not need.)

1 ☐ Healthy lifestyles
2 ☐ *A* An American experiment
3 ☐ A changed man
4 ☐ A film diary
5 ☐ A shorter experiment

**2** Answer the questions. Use full sentences.

How many months did Spurlock's experiment last?
*His experiment lasted for one month.*

1 How did Spurlock record his experiences?
_____
_____

2 How did Spurlock feel at the end of the month?
_____
_____

3 When did Adams do his experiment and how long did it last?
_____
_____

4 How did eating fast food change Adams' health?
_____
_____

5 What happened to Adams' character?
_____
_____

# Grammar

## Past simple or past continuous?

**1** Complete the dialogue with the phrases in the box.

> ~~didn't do~~   Did they mention   Did you leave
> didn't know   gave   was trying   wasn't listening
> were planning   were you doing
> were they talking   were

Jack   I *didn't do* my English homework last night.
Chris   (1) _____ your book at
         school?
Jack   No, I (2) _____ which
         exercises to do.
Chris   Why not? You (3) _____
         in the lesson yesterday.
Jack   Yes, but I (4) _____
         when Miss Jones (5) _____
         us our homework.
Chris   What (6) _____?
Jack   I (7) _____ to listen to
         Anna and Sarah.
Chris   Why? What (8) _____
         about?
Jack   They (9) _____ a picnic.
Chris   Really? (10) _____ our
         names?
Jack   No, they didn't!

**2** Complete the questions. Use the past simple or past continuous form of the verbs in brackets.

1   What time *did you get up* (you / get up) today?
2   Where _____ (you / be) at
     eight o'clock this morning?
3   _____ (the bus / arrive) late?
4   _____
     (the other students / work) at that time?
5   What _____ (you / say) to the
     teacher?

**3** Match questions 1–5 in exercise 2 with answers a–e. Then complete the sentences with the past simple or past continuous form of the verbs in brackets.

a ☐ Yes, they _____ (have) a
     maths lesson.
b ☐ Yes. And I _____
     (not arrive) at school until nine!
c ☐ I _____ (wait) at the bus
     stop.
d ☐ I was very polite. I _____
     (say) 'Sorry'.
e ☒ I *got up* (get up) at seven o'clock.

**4** Write sentences. Use the past simple or past continuous form of the verbs.

> when / the teacher / ask / me a question / I /
> not listen
> *When the teacher asked me a question,*
> *I wasn't listening.*

1   it / start / raining / while / we / wait / for the bus
     _____
     _____
2   Max / watch / a DVD / when / he / fall / asleep
     _____
     _____
3   who / you / see / while / you / walk /
     home yesterday / ?
     _____
     _____
4   I / not go / to school / yesterday / because / I /
     swim / in a competition
     _____
     _____
5   while / Kate / do / her homework / she /
     receive / a text message
     _____
     _____
6   your parents / have / dinner / when / they /
     hear / the news / ?
     _____
     _____

**5** Correct the mistake in each sentence.

Were you enjoying your holiday last summer?
*Did you enjoy your holiday last summer?*

1 The phone rang while I listened to some music.

_____

_____

2 They were having dinner when I was arriving.

_____

_____

3 It's 10.30 and the lesson was starting at 10.15.

_____

_____

4 Everybody was talking when the teacher was coming in.

_____

_____

# Infinitive of purpose

**6** Write complete sentences with the phrases in boxes A and B.

A  ~~use mobile phones~~  do exercise
read newspapers  use buses  go to picnics
go to supermarkets  wear coats

B  be sociable  ~~contact each other~~
find out the news  buy food  keep fit
stay warm  travel to places

People *use mobile phones to contact each other.*

1 People _____

_____

2 _____

_____

3 _____

_____

4 _____

_____

5 _____

_____

6 _____

_____

**7** Write sentences with the past simple and an infinitive of purpose.

I / go / to the kitchen / make / a drink
*I went to the kitchen to make a drink.*

1 we / wait / at the station / catch / a train

_____

_____

2 Jim / borrow / my phone / ring / Fran

_____

_____

3 he / go / to the cinema / see / a film

_____

_____

4 they / go / to the shop / buy / a DVD

_____

_____

5 I / buy / flowers / give / my Mum

_____

_____

# Consolidation

**8** Complete the text with the phrases in the box.

didn't know  found  looked  said  spent
to look for  to say  was looking  was sitting
~~was studying~~  went

My elder brother, Lucas, is really shy. When he
was *studying* at Nottingham University, he
(1) _____ many people and
he never (2) _____ out with
friends. He was very hard-working and he always
(3) _____ a lot of time at the
library. One day, Lucas went to the library
(4) _____ some information for
a project. While he (5) _____
at the internet, he (6) _____
an interesting website called, 'How to be more
outgoing'. It (7) _____,
'Find a cheerful person and say hello.'

Lucas (8) _____ around. He
(9) _____ near a girl, so he
walked over (10) _____ hello to her.
Her name was Mary and they are now married!

# Communication

## Vocabulary  Character adjectives

**1** Complete the puzzle. What is the mystery character adjective?

```
¹P A T I E N T
        ²
        ³
      ⁴
    ⁵
  ⁶
    ⁷
      ⁸
  ⁹
```

The mystery character adjective is _____.

1  A _____ person doesn't mind waiting.
2  The opposite of generous.
3  The opposite of rude.
4  The opposite of hard-working.
5  The opposite of shy.
6  The opposite of silly.
7  Another adjective for happy.
8  An _____ person doesn't lie.
9  A _____ person thinks about other people's feelings.

**2** Complete the sentences with adjectives from the puzzle in exercise 1.

What's the matter? You don't look very *cheerful*.
1  My brother isn't very _____. He always does silly things.
2  It's _____ to always say please and thank you.
3  Lara gets up late every day. She's very _____.
4  Please be _____ and tell me the truth.
5  Dan is _____. He never gives me any chocolate.
6  'Hurry up!' 'Wait a moment. Please be _____!'
7  Don't shout at Lucy! She's really _____.

## *give* and *make*

**3** Match 1–8 with a–h to make complete sentences.

1  [d] The baby is asleep. Don't make ...
2  [ ] Dad was angry. He gave us a final ...
3  [ ] You were late. Did you give the teacher ...
4  [ ] This book is great. It gives really clear ...
5  [ ] Paula is sensible. She always gives ...
6  [ ] I'm not sure. I haven't made a ...
7  [ ] That isn't the answer. Let me make ...
8  [ ] Joe is selling his bike. I've got enough money, so I've made ...

a  examples.
b  warning.
c  an offer.
d  any noise!
e  decision yet.
f  good advice.
g  a good explanation?
h  a suggestion.

## Speaking  New friends

**4** Put the conversation in the correct order.

a  [ ] That's Elena. She's from Greece.

b  [ ] I was giving her some advice. She's feeling miserable because she doesn't know many people.

c  [1] Who's that girl you were talking to?

d  [ ] That's a great idea! I'll go and ask her now.

e  [ ] Really? And what were you talking about?

f  [ ] I know! Why doesn't she come to the youth club on Friday?

g  [ ] She's staying here for a month to learn English and I decided to talk to her.

h  [ ] Greece? So what's she doing in Manchester?!

# Writing

## A postcard  Capital letters

**1** Write the sentences with the correct capital letters.

i met tom while i was studying in italy.
*I met Tom while I was studying in Italy.*

1 the british love visiting spain in summer.

_____

_____

2 'when is your birthday?' 'it's in february.'

_____

_____

3 'is sara american?' 'no, she's from england.'

_____

_____

4 laura and james speak french.

_____

5 did they send you a postcard from biarritz?

_____

_____

6 we went skiing in the mountains in january.

_____

_____

**2** Complete the postcard with the expressions in the box. Use the past simple or past continuous form of the verbs.

sun / shine   cycle / back   ~~meet / a French family~~   borrow / the family's bikes   make / lots of good suggestions
not swim / for long   visit / a spectacular place

Dear Amanda

We're staying in a beautiful village in France. We *met a French family* when we
arrived. They were very friendly and they (1) _____
about places to visit. Thanks to them, we (2) _____
in the mountains. We walked for about half an hour and found a small lake. It was
hot and the (3) _____, so we decided to have a swim. We
(4) _____ because the water was freezing!

Yesterday, we (5) _____ and went cycling.
We cycled about 20 kilometres, but it felt like 40! The weather wasn't great. It
started raining while we (6) _____ to the
hotel and we got really wet!

Mr and Mrs
44 Southfie
Oxford
OX4 1XR

**3** Write the end of the postcard. Use capital letters and full stops where necessary.

*The people in the village don't speak much English,* _____

_____

_____

_____

_____

the people in the village don't speak much english, so our french is getting better lisa
and tom are going to buy some souvenirs tomorrow there's a big market on wednesdays
which sells lots of french products

see you on saturday

love, sue xxx

# Quick check

## Vocabulary

**1** Complete the text with the correct character adjectives.

When somebody gives you a strange present, is it
(1) r_____ and (2) i_____ to say
that you don't like it? Should you be
(3) p_____ and say, 'How lovely! It's very
(4) g_____ of you!' because you don't want
to hurt the person's feelings? Or is it kinder to be
completely (5) h_____ and explain in a
(6) s_____ way that you can't imagine
using it?

**2** Choose the correct answer.

1 We made a **noise / decision** and the baby woke up.
2 Did you **give / make** a clear explanation?
3 Did they **make / give** you a good offer?
4 Did she **give / make** you an example?
5 I enjoy **giving / making** people advice.
6 My teacher gave us a **confession / warning**.

## Vocabulary review

**3** Complete the sentences with the words in the box.

> advice   cheerful   hard-working   impatient
> offers   warning

1 A life coach is somebody who gives you
   _____ about improving your life.
2 Optimistic people often feel _____ as well.
3 They passed all their exams because they were so
   _____.
4 Nobody made any _____ of help, so I
   did it alone.
5 We're coming. Don't be so _____!
6 The weather programme gave a _____
   about the snow.

## Grammar

**4** Complete the sentences. Use the past simple or past continuous form of the verbs in brackets.

1 We _____ (have) dinner when
   the baby _____ (start) crying.
2 Antonio _____ (meet) his wife
   while he _____ (work) there.
3 _____ (she / cycle) when you
   _____ (see) her?
4 'Why _____ (you / leave)?'
   'I _____ (not enjoy) myself.'
5 Mark _____ (listen) to a CD
   when I _____ (call) him.

**5** Complete the sentences with the verbs in the box. Use the infinitive of purpose.

> answer   buy   do   invite   make

1 I phoned Julie _____ her to
   my party.
2 Nick put up his hand _____ a
   question.
3 They joined a club _____ new
   friends.
4 Do you use the internet _____
   your homework?
5 Let's go shopping _____
   Lucy's present!

## Grammar review

**6** Choose the correct answer.

Ben is often late for school. Yesterday, for example,
he (1) **walked / was walking** down the road when
the school bus (2) **went / was going** past him. He
ran (3) **catch / to catch** it, but he (4) **didn't get /
wasn't getting** to the bus stop in time.

When Ben finally (5) **arrived / was arriving** at school,
his teacher gave him a present. 'It's something
(6) **help / to help** you get to school on time,'
explained Ms Martin. Ben (7) **was opening / opened**
the present and (8) **started / was starting**
to laugh. It was a very big alarm clock!

**12** UNIT I

# 2 Sport

## Reading

# Footballers of the future

**A** David Beckham has opened his own sports academy which will teach football to more than 10,000 children aged eight–fifteen each year. Beckham himself will even give the luckiest of those children some personal footballing advice.

**B** The David Beckham Academy, in Greenwich, east London, is the biggest sports academy in Europe. It has two indoor football pitches, classrooms, a dining hall and medical facilities. Beckham wants the academy to give children a fun and safe alternative to playing football in the street. Children can visit the academy on school trips, and in the school holidays there are football courses which last 3 to 5 days.

**C** Beckham was born in east London on 2 May 1975 and he was good at football from an early age. He practised at the Bobby Charlton Soccer School, where he won a special award at the age of eleven. Bobby Charlton played for Manchester United in the 1950s and 1960s, and he helped England to win the World Cup in 1966.

**D** David Beckham joined Manchester United as a trainee in 1991 and he played for United professionally from 1993. Then, in 2003, he moved to Real Madrid, before joining Los Angeles Galaxy in 2007. But he has never forgotten Charlton. In fact, his experiences have inspired him to establish his own academy.

**E** As Beckham doesn't live in England, he cannot go to the academy every day, but he has promised to visit regularly. He has made all of the decisions about the academy and he has chosen Eric Harrison, who trained the youth teams at United, to be the head coach. Beckham is now planning a second academy, this time in Los Angeles.

**1** Read the text and put the events into the correct order.

a ☐ Beckham moved to Real Madrid.
b ☐ England won the World Cup.
c ☐ Beckham opened a sporting academy.
d ☐ 1 Charlton joined Manchester United.
e ☐ Beckham joined Manchester United.
f ☐ Beckham was born in London.
g ☐ Beckham joined a football academy.

**2** Answer the questions. Use full sentences.

What is Beckham's ambition for the new academy?
*He wants it to teach children about football in a safe and fun environment.*

1 Who can go to the academy and when can they go?
_____
_____

2 How long was Beckham a professional player at Manchester United?
_____
_____

3 Does Beckham still like Bobby Charlton? How do you know?
_____
_____
_____

4 Beckham does not teach at the academy full-time. Why not?
_____
_____

5 How has Beckham influenced what the academy is like?
_____
_____

# Grammar

## Present perfect (1)

**1** Complete the interview. Use the present perfect form of the verbs in brackets.

**Teen Focus** has interviewed (interview) future sports star, Kate Standring, to find out about her love of swimming.

**TF**   Hi, Kate. It's seven o'clock in the morning and you _____ (**1** finish) a two-hour training session. How far _____ (**2** you / swim)?

**Kate**   I _____ (**3** do) 200 lengths, which is 5 km.

**TF**   Incredible! What's the hardest thing about the training sessions?

**Kate**   Getting up so early in the morning is very difficult, but I _____ (**4** not miss) a session!

**TF**   How long _____ (**5** you / train) here?

**Kate**   Hmm. I _____ (**6** forget). I think it's about four years.

**TF**   Do you swim in competitions?

**Kate**   Yes, the club _____ (**7** compete) in six competitions this year. I've got lots of cups and medals at home!

**TF**   Have you got a hero?

**Kate**   Yes. Ian Thorpe, the Australian swimmer. He _____ (**8** win) five Olympic gold medals and that's what I'd love to do one day!

**2** Write the words in the correct order.

had / you / have / a good time / ?
*Have you had a good time?*

1   he / money / has / spent / much / how / ?

_____

_____

2   Ronaldinho / we / 've / twice / met

_____

3   ridden / a motorbike / I / haven't

_____

4   you / have / bought / today / any souvenirs / ?

_____

_____

5   my team / won / this year / a match / hasn't

_____

_____

**3** Complete the questions. Use the present perfect form of the verbs in the box.

> he / collect   Elena / cycle   your brother / have
> Paul / watch   she / play   you / visit

1   *Has she played* a lot of football?
2   How long _____ a season ticket for Liverpool?
3   How many times _____ that film?
4   Why _____ to school this week?
5   _____ many countries?
6   How many wristbands _____?

**4** Complete the answers with the present perfect form of the verbs in brackets. Then match them with questions 1–6 in exercise 3.

a   ☐ Fifteen. He _____ (find) most of them on the internet.
b   ☐ Because she _____ (decide) to get fit.
c   ☐ Five years, and he _____ (not miss) a game!
d   ☐ Yes, I have. I _____ (visit) lots of places in Europe and Asia.
e   ☐ 1 No, she's played (play) three games, I think.
f   ☐ Ten. He _____ (buy) it on DVD.

## been or gone?

**5** **Complete the sentences with *been* or *gone*.**

You're late! Where have you *been*?

1  We've _____ to the cinema twice this week.
2  'Has she _____ to bed?' 'Yes, it's midnight.'
3  Nobody is here. They've all _____ home.
4  How many countries have you _____ to?
5  Where are we? I haven't _____ here before.
6  She's _____ swimming. She'll be back later.

## ever and never

**6** **Write the sentences with *ever* or *never*.**

she / watch / the Tour de France  **?**
*Has she ever watched the Tour de France?*

1  that was the best match / they / play  ✓
   _____
   _____

2  you / play / rugby  **?**
   _____

3  he / compete / in the Olympic Games  **?**
   _____
   _____

4  you / run / a marathon  ✗
   _____

5  this is the hardest thing / they / do  ✓
   _____
   _____

6  I / collect / souvenirs  ✗
   _____

## Consolidation

**7** **Correct the mistake in each sentence.**

We haven't never learnt how to swim.
*We have never learnt how to swim.*

1  'You look well.' 'I've gone on holiday.'
   _____

2  Have they ever weared wristbands?
   _____

3  'Has you seen Mary?' 'No, I haven't.'
   _____

4  We haven't ran 400 metres before.
   _____

5  I never heard of that footballer.
   _____

6  'Where's John?' 'He's been to school.'
   _____

**8** **Complete the text with the verbs in the box.**

> has he learnt   's decided   's brought   has read
> 's travelled   has done   ~~have you ever done~~
> 've collected   've never been   hasn't forgotten

*Have you ever done* anything silly? Well, sixteen-year-old Oscar Beech (**1**) _____ something completely mad. He's a huge fan of Ronaldinho and he (**2**) _____ 350 miles from his home in Scotland to see his hero. Oscar (**3**) _____ in the newspaper that Ronaldinho is coming to London tomorrow to receive a special award. He (**4**) _____ to wait outside the hotel to see the football star when he arrives. 'I don't live in Barcelona, so I (**5**) _____ _____ to any matches at Nou Camp,' he explained, 'but I (**6**) _____ a lot of photos and articles about Ronaldinho.' Oscar is wearing a Barcelona football shirt which he wants Ronaldinho to autograph. He (**7**) _____ anything – he (**8**) _____ an indelible marker pen with him, but (**9**) _____ how to say 'Hello' in Portuguese?

# Communication

## Vocabulary Sport

**1** Label the photographs.

1  slope          4  p_____
2  b_____    5  g_____
3  s_____

6  r_____    8  c_____
7  b_____    9  t_____

## *do, go* and *play*

**2** Complete the sentences with *do, go* or *play*.

Let's *go* ice-skating!
1  Did he _____ a triathlon?
2  Jake can't _____ volleyball because he's hurt his hand.
3  My sisters _____ karate twice a week.
4  A lot of people _____ windsurfing in summer.
5  When did you _____ squash for the first time?
6  I don't _____ gymnastics.
7  Why don't you _____ jogging every morning?
8  We _____ horse riding every year.

## Speaking  Football fans

**3** Complete the dialogue with the words in the box.

> net  play  ~~match~~  boots  cap  fan  stadium
> pitch  team

**Sara**  Oh, no! Rob's gone to watch a football *match* at Old Trafford and he's forgotten his (1) _____.

**Jack**  It doesn't matter.

**Sara**  You don't understand. He always wears it when Manchester United (2) _____ at home.

**Jack**  Has he always supported the same (3) _____?

**Sara**  Yes, I think he's United's biggest (4) _____! He's been on a tour of the (5) _____ about twenty times.

**Jack**  Twenty times! Why?

**Sara**  Because you can put on a pair of (6) _____ and run onto the (7) _____! Rob loves it, and each time he imagines kicking the ball into the back of the (8) _____!

# Writing

## A biography   Linking words

**1**  Complete the sentences with *but*, *however*, *and*, *also* or *so*.

I did judo for the first time yesterday, *but* I didn't enjoy it.

1  Pete is really good at tennis. He's _____ an amazing squash player.

2  Emma was tired, _____ she didn't go swimming.

3  Sport is good for you. It's _____ great fun.

4  He plays tennis _____ he's a good footballer, too.

5  John doesn't like football. _____, he went to a match with Rick.

6  They speak Turkish _____ they've never been to Turkey.

7  We want to get fit, _____ we go jogging every day.

**2**  Complete the biography with the information in the box.

across the road   doctors   started the first Arabic newspaper
Tunisia   ~~Selima Sfar~~   when she was only thirteen

### Selima Sfar

*Selima Sfar* is known as the best Arab women's tennis player in the world. She was born on 8 July 1977 in Sidi Bou Saïd, in northern (1) _____. Her grandfather, a famous journalist, (2) _____ in Tunisia. Both her mother and father are (3) _____. Selima started playing tennis after school in a local club (4) _____ from her house, so her parents didn't worry about her. She was already the best tennis player in the country (5) _____.

**3**  Complete the end of the biography. Use the past simple (PS) or present perfect (PP) form of the verbs in brackets, and the linking words in the box.

and   but   ~~so~~   however

Selima's grandfather wanted her to continue her tennis education, (1) *so* her parents (2 send PS) _____ her to France to study. She (3 live PP) _____ for a long time (4) _____ she never forgets her family and her home in Tunisia. She (5 start PS) _____ playing professionally in 1999 (6) _____ she (7 win PP) _____ many international tournaments. She wants to open a special sports school one day. (8) _____, there (9 be PP) _____ enough time for that yet – 'maybe in one or two years', she says.

## Quick check

## Vocabulary

**1** **Complete the sentences with words for sport places and equipment.**

1 The athletes walked around the t_____ before the race.
2 Jim can't come. He's lost his swimming t_____.
3 I kicked the ball onto the p_____.
4 People wear g_____ to protect their eyes.
5 Have you seen Linda's new swimming c_____?
6 It's a goal! The ball is in the n_____.

**2** **Choose the correct answer.**

1 We **did / played** judo at school today.
2 I've never **done / been** horse riding.
3 Where does Mark **go / play** golf?
4 Americans love **playing / doing** baseball.
5 Alice **does / goes** jogging every morning.
6 Have you ever **played / done** athletics?

## Vocabulary review: Units 1–2

**3** **Complete the sentences with the words in the box.**

> cycling  gives  ice-skating  makes  miserable
> poles  rackets  rude

1 Professional tennis players use several _____ in a match.
2 The footballer left the pitch because he was _____ to the referee.
3 Triathletes are good at swimming, _____ and running.
4 She usually _____ a warning.
5 Alex looks _____ because he's lost an important match.
6 In New York, you can go _____ outdoors in winter.
7 I lost one of my _____ when I went skiing yesterday.
8 Your motorbike _____ a lot of noise.

## Grammar

**4** **Complete the sentences. Use the present perfect form of the verbs in the box.**

> you / collect  not do  play  you / read
> not start  walk

1 Most football coaches _____ football professionally.
2 How many cards _____?
3 The girls _____ judo before.
4 Don't worry, the match _____.
5 Yes, we _____ 15 km before.
6 _____ that book?

**5** **Complete the sentences with *ever*, *never*, *been* or *gone*.**

1 I've _____ enjoyed doing athletics.
2 We haven't _____ to America.
3 You're wet. Have you _____ swimming?
4 He's the best footballer I've _____ seen.
5 Sally isn't here. She's _____ cycling.
6 Have they _____ done a triathlon?

## Grammar review: Units 1–2

**6** **Choose the correct answers.**

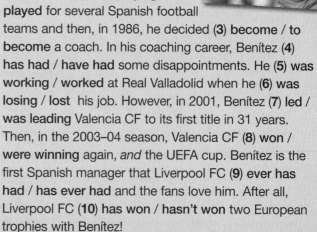

### Rafael Benítez

Rafael Benítez, the manager of Liverpool Football Club, **(1) joined / was joining** the club in 2004. He **(2) was playing / played** for several Spanish football teams and then, in 1986, he decided **(3) become / to become** a coach. In his coaching career, Benítez **(4) has had / have had** some disappointments. He **(5) was working / worked** at Real Valladolid when he **(6) was losing / lost** his job. However, in 2001, Benítez **(7) led / was leading** Valencia CF to its first title in 31 years. Then, in the 2003–04 season, Valencia CF **(8) won / were winning** again, *and* the UEFA cup. Benítez is the first Spanish manager that Liverpool FC **(9) ever has had / has ever had** and the fans love him. After all, Liverpool FC **(10) has won / hasn't won** two European trophies with Benítez!

# 3 | Architecture

## Living on water

**A** Most homes are near a road because most of us use roads to get around. In some places, boats are more useful than cars, so living near a river is more important. But wherever we live, we all want to live in a house on dry land, don't we?

**B** Not always! For thousands of years, some people have done exactly the opposite: they have built their homes on water instead of land. Millions of people in Asia actually live on lakes, not just near lakes. Their homes are huts on stilts.

**C** In parts of Cambodia, people even live in floating huts. Why? Heavy rainfall causes floods, and floods destroy thousands of conventional huts every year. But too much rainwater is never a problem for floating homes because they float, just like a boat. At Inle Lake in Burma, they even have floating gardens. Floating gardens are good because there is always plenty of water for the plants.

**D** Living on water is not as popular in Europe, but there are still thousands of canal 'narrowboats' in the UK. A canal is a man-made waterway – Suez and Panama are famous examples of canals. People have used narrowboats on the British canal network since the 1750s, both as a means of transport and as a home. They are only two metres wide and 15–20 metres long, so they can sail along narrow canals. Some people live in narrowboats all of the year, but most are holiday homes these days.

---

**1** Read the text. Are the sentences true or false? Explain your answers.

Rivers are more important than roads.
*False. Most people travel on roads, not rivers.*

1 Everybody wants a house on dry land.

2 Huts are common on rivers.

3 Canals are not natural structures.

4 Narrowboats are popular on the Suez Canal.

5 A narrowboat is a type of villa.

**2** Answer the questions. Use full sentences.

What is close to most homes?
*Most homes are near a road.*

1 What type of home is typical in some parts of Asia?

2 What is different about some Cambodian huts?

3 What is the advantage of a floating hut?

4 What is the advantage of a floating garden?

5 Why are narrowboats narrow?

# Grammar

## Present perfect (2) *for* or *since*?

**1 Complete the phrases with *for* or *since*.**

*Since* Monday

1 _____ ten minutes     5 _____ two months
2 _____ last summer     6 _____ a day
3 _____ I was young     7 _____ the 1990s
4 _____ yesterday       8 _____ years

**2 Write sentences or questions with the present perfect and *for* or *since*.**

Alan / practise / the violin / seven years ✓
*Alan has practised the violin for seven years.*

1 I / speak / to Kim / her birthday ✗

_____

_____

2 you / study / English / many years ?

_____

3 she / design / skyscrapers / 25 years ✓

_____

4 he / live / in Southampton / he was nine ✓

_____

5 we / ride / our bikes / a long time ✗

_____

_____

6 they / know / each other / 2004 ?

_____

_____

**3 Rewrite the sentences. Use the present perfect and *for* or *since*.**

I live in Leeds. I moved here in September. (since)
*I've lived in Leeds since September.*

1 They started studying English five years ago. (for)

_____

_____

2 She doesn't do karate any more. She stopped doing it last month. (for)

_____

_____

3 We're in a maths lesson. It started at ten o'clock. (since)

_____

_____

4 He plays tennis. He started playing it when he was five. (since)

_____

_____

## *already* or *yet*?

**4 Put the words in the correct order.**

started / programme / yet / the / has / ?
*Has the programme started yet?*

1 emailed / you / already / your friends / have / ?

_____

2 they / already / have / on holiday / this year / been

_____

3 haven't / the / they / yet / building / finished

_____

4 yet / your parents / you / have / spoken to / ?

_____

5 the piano / I / practised / today / already / have

_____

6 present / haven't / we / Simon's / bought / yet

_____

_____

**5** **Rewrite the sentences. Use the present perfect and *already* or *yet*.**

We (not finish) the walls. (yet)
*We haven't finished the walls yet.*

1 The architects (design) two towers. (already)

_____

2 I (visit) Burj al-Arab. (already)

_____

3 (you / see) the Great Pyramid? (yet)

_____

4 They (not finish) the palm islands. (yet)

_____

5 (he / buy) the insulating material? (already)

_____

6 The straw for the roof (not arrive). (yet)

_____

## *just*

**6** **Complete the sentences with the verbs in the box. Use the present perfect and *just*.**

| finish | go | ~~laugh~~ | cut | start | surf | win |

'Why is Ruth laughing?' '*I've just told* her a joke.'

1 Tom _____ his finger, but he'll be OK.

2 Everybody is excited because we _____ the World Cup.

3 I _____ the internet.

4 You can't speak to Mark. He _____ to bed.

5 Sara _____ learning the guitar.

6 Everybody is leaving because the match _____ .

## Consolidation

**7** **Correct the mistake in each sentence.**

My family has lived here since a long time.
*My family has lived here for a long time.*

1 They haven't stealed anything yet.

_____

2 That man has been just very rude.

_____

3 Have you yet done this exercise?

_____

4 We hasn't spoken to each other for days.

_____

5 I haven't gone to the beach for May.

_____

6 You just have finished this book?

_____

**8** **Complete the text with *for*, *since*, *just*, *already* or *yet*.**

I've worked at Stockhomes *for* seven years and I specialise in towers. We designed several towers for a German bank in 2003, and we've designed about ten towers **(1)** _____ then. In fact, we've **(2)** _____ finished the second of the three Stadmanton Towers. They opened the building this morning!

I love towers, but I'm a bit nervous about Tower III. Nobody has built a 400-metre tower **(3)** _____! We haven't started the walls for Tower III **(4)** _____, but we've **(5)** _____ prepared the ground, and that's the most important part of the building. **(6)** _____ I started at Stockhomes, I've learnt that preparation is everything.

# Communication

## Vocabulary  Buildings and structures

**1** Complete the crossword.

```
    ¹B R I D G E
    ²
          ³
    ⁴
          ⁵
      ⁶
    ⁷
```

### Across (→)
1  For going across a river.
2  Where ships collect and leave goods.
4  A very tall building.
5  For travelling underneath things.
6  Where you can go shopping.
7  A fast road with a lot of cars.

### Down (↓)
1  A building with flats in it.
3  Where kings and queens live.

## Negative prefixes

**2** Complete the table with the adjectives in the box.

adventurous afraid conventional experienced
formal original personal possible practical

| im- | in- | un- |
|-----|-----|-----|
|     |     | adventurous |
|     |     |     |
|     |     |     |
|     |     |     |

**3** Complete the sentences with the adjectives in exercise 2.

Don't worry! It's an *informal* discussion.
1  They never try anything new. They're so
   _____.
2  Emailing is more _____ than
   writing letters.
3  It's a bit _____ to take a bike
   on the train.
4  I've heard all his jokes before. He's really
   _____.
5  I'm very _____. I've only
   worked here for a day.

## Speaking  Double Decker Living

**4** Match a–d with 1–4 in the dialogue.

Ed   Have you heard of Double Decker Living?
Sal  (1) ____
Ed   They've converted double-decker London
     buses into homes!
Sal  (2) ____
Ed   To recycle buses, and to provide cheap
     accommodation.
Sal  (3) ____
Ed   They're modern and comfortable.
Sal  (4) ____

a  What are they like inside?
b  Really? Why have the done that?
c  Maybe we can stay in a Double Decker hotel in
   London!
d  No. What's that?

# Writing

## An interview   Ordering ideas

**1** Complete the questions. Use the present perfect (PP) or the past simple (PS) form of the verbs in brackets.

What *have you found* (you / find) for us this week? (PP)

1   And how _____ (you / get into) the sphere? (PS)

2   Next, why _____ (the sphere / be) so popular? (PP)

3   Finally, why _____ (they / put) this sphere in a forest? (PP)

4   First of all, why _____ (you / choose) the Free Spirit Sphere? (PP)

5   Secondly, how _____ (they / make) the sphere? (PS)

**2** Complete the interview with the questions from exercise 1.

**ArchiMag**   Welcome, Tom. *What have you found for us this week?*

**Tom Cox**   This is a Free Spirit Sphere. It's a sphere – or ball – with one room inside.

**ArchiMag**   (a) _____

**Tom Cox**   I chose it because it's so simple. It's only got two walls, there's one wall inside and the other wall is the outside.

**ArchiMag**   (b) _____

**Tom Cox**   The sphere is wooden, and it hangs from ropes between three tall trees.

**ArchiMag**   (c) _____

**Tom Cox**   I used a ladder and then a rope bridge to get into it.

**ArchiMag**   (d) _____

**Tom Cox**   Spheres are the perfect place to read books, listen to music and watch DVDs. And they're a really original design, as well.

**ArchiMag**   (e) _____

**Tom Cox**   Well, you can relax at home, but for real relaxation you need to escape from the city. I'd recommend a Free Spirit Sphere to anybody!

# Quick check

## Vocabulary

**1** Complete the sentences with words for buildings and structures.

1 The m_____ doesn't go near Rome.
2 Cross the road on the b_____ .
3 The m_____ opens at ten.
4 His office is at the top of this s_____ .
5 It was dark in the t_____ .
6 There aren't any houses, but there's a b_____ of f_____ .

**2** Which word is not correct in each group (buildings or structures)?

1 block of flats   castle   skyscraper   tunnel
2 bridge   monument   mall   motorway
3 castle   monument   port   tunnel

**3** Choose the correct negative prefix.

1 inexperienced / imexperienced
2 unadventurous / inadventurous
3 unpractical / impractical
4 inoriginal / unoriginal
5 informal / unformal
6 impersonal / inpersonal

## Vocabulary review: Units 1–3

**4** Complete the sentences with the words in the box.

> done   given   impractical   made   sensible
> sensitive   slope   unconventional

1 He's an _____ and very original designer.
2 There's a new ski _____ in Dubai.
3 My brother has never _____ karate.
4 She's _____ us some advice.
5 Skis are _____ for walking.
6 Gina seems older than ten. She's so _____.
7 Have you _____ a decision yet?
8 That story was beautiful. The writer is a very _____ person.

## Grammar

**5** Complete the sentences with the present perfect and *for* or *since*.

1 I _____ (not play) squash _____ weeks.
2 He _____ (design) bridges _____ three years.
3 We _____ (not go) horse riding _____ we were young.
4 'How long _____ (you / live) here?' '_____ two months.'
5 Tom _____ (be) at this school _____ 2005.
6 I _____ (wait) for you _____ 45 minutes.

**6** Choose the correct answer.

1 'You look tired.' 'I've **just** / **already** been jogging.'
2 She hasn't read that book **already** / **yet**.
3 He's shy because he's **already** / **just** joined the club.
4 Have you had any juice **just** / **yet**?
5 I'm not hungry. I've **yet** / **already** eaten.
6 Have they **yet** / **just** been to the beach?

## Grammar review: Units 1–3

**7** Choose the correct answer.

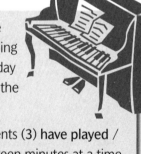

(1) **Did** / **Have** you ever done anything for charity? We're doing a 'pianothon' at my school today (2) **to raise** / **raise** money for the Earthquake Appeal.

It's ten o'clock. Different students (3) **have played** / **were playing** the piano for fifteen minutes at a time (4) **for** / **since** nine o'clock. We're going to continue for another three hours! I (5) **'ve** / **haven't** had my turn (6) **yet** / **already**, so I'm feeling rather nervous.

My friend, Joe, (7) **just finished** / **has just finished** playing. I (8) **asked** / **was asking** him what it was like. 'There (9) **were** / **was** so many people in the hall,' he said. 'It felt like I (10) **gave** / **was giving** a huge concert!'

# Revision: Units 1-3

## Vocabulary

**1** Complete the crossword.

**Down (↓)**
1 Not optimistic.
2 Not unique.
3 Unhappy.
4 Not serious.
7 Not outgoing.

**Across (→)**
5 Brave.
6 Not easy.
8 Not sensible.
9 Not hard-working.

**2** Complete the sentences with sports words.

1 You can't play t_____ without a ball!
2 We're running on the new t_____ today.
3 Take your s_____ costume and I'll meet you at the p_____.
4 How high is the n_____ on a badminton c_____?
5 You don't need p_____ for snowboarding.
6 Are those f_____ boots new?
7 I always wear g_____ for swimming.
8 Can I wear these t_____ to go running?

**3** Complete the sentences with *give, make, do, go* and *play*.

1 How often does Sally _____ squash?
2 Do you think the man will _____ a confession?
3 I _____ jogging every morning.
4 She didn't _____ a very good explanation.
5 Can I _____ a suggestion?
6 We don't want to _____ rugby.
7 Rita and Jan _____ a triathlon every year.
8 They walked onto the court to _____ tennis.

**4** Complete the sentences with the words in the box.

> cheerful generous goggles inexperienced impossible mall miserable order outgoing pitch racket sensible slope suggestions

1 I was skiing down the _____ when my _____ fell off!
2 The referee gave an _____: 'Don't argue on the football _____.'
3 Although Katy is _____, she's already designed a _____.
4 The architect made some _____ _____.
5 Paul is very _____. He's just given me a new tennis _____.
6 You need to be _____ and _____ to make friends.
7 The test was _____. I feel really _____ now.

# Grammar

**1** Complete the sentences. Use the past simple or past continuous form of the verbs in brackets .

1 I _____ (not speak) to Lucy because I _____ (do) my homework.

2 '_____ (you / have) dinner when I _____ (phone)?' 'Yes, we were.'

3 Kelly _____ (not make) many friends while she _____ (study) at college.

4 We _____ (watch) a DVD when our neighbour _____ (knock) on the door.

5 He _____ (lose) his phone while he _____ (run) to the park.

6 It _____ (rain) when the football match _____ (start).

**2** Write sentences with the past simple and the infinitive of purpose.

1 we / go / to Dubai / practise / skiing

_____

_____

2 they / join / the club / make / new friends / ?

_____

_____

3 my parents / go / to a café / have / a meal

_____

_____

4 I / wait / outside school / meet / Kevin

_____

_____

5 she / wear / goggles / protect / her eyes

_____

_____

6 he / speak / to the teacher / get / some advice

_____

_____

7 you / go / to the park / play / football / ?

_____

_____

**3** Complete the interview with the present perfect form of the verbs in brackets.

**Sport FM** The England cricket team are back in the UK today. They _____ (1 just / finish) a two-week tour of India and Pakistan. Sport FM reporter, Jez Duncan, _____ (2 go) to the airport to meet the team. Jez, _____ (3 you / see) the team yet?

**Duncan** Well, hundreds and hundreds of fans _____ (4 come) to the airport to welcome the players home. Everybody _____ (5 be) really patient. It's a hot day and we _____ (6 wait) for an hour so far. The players' plane _____ (7 already / land), but nobody _____ (8 walk) through the doors yet. Wait! Here's Andrew Flintoff, the captain. Andrew, how was the tour?

**Flintoff** Amazing! It was definitely the best tour we _____ (9 ever / do), but it's good to be home again!

**4** Complete the sentences. Use the present perfect form of the verbs in the box.

> they / eat   you / know   learn   not make
> finish   not score

1 Talal _____ any goals yet.
2 How long _____ each other?
3 I _____ English since I was a child.
4 How much chocolate _____?
5 We _____ a mistake yet.
6 You can use my computer. I _____ my essay.

**5** Complete the text with the words in the box.

> already   ever   for   just   never   since   yet

What's the longest book you've
(**1**) _____ read?

I've (**2**) _____ finished reading
*Treasure Island* (about five minutes ago!). There are 88 pages in it, but it only took two hours to read it. I've tried reading books in English before, but I've (**3**) _____ finished them. However, this time it wasn't difficult. I haven't read such a good book (**4**) _____ a long time. I've loved adventure stories ever (**5**) _____ I was young. I haven't read any other stories by Robert Louis Stevenson (**6**) _____, but I've (**7**) _____ borrowed *Kidnapped* from the school library!

**6** Correct the mistake in each sentence.

1 We often go to the cinema for to watch a film.
_____

2 I haven't never eaten fast food.
_____

3 What was you doing when the phone rang?
_____

4 Chris isn't here because he's been swimming.
_____

5 They were seeing a friend while they were jogging.
_____

6 My parents didn't meet my teacher yet.
_____

**7** Complete the text with the words in the box.

> has done   have just joined   have never done
> haven't bought   saw   to ask   to get   've always
> been   was looking   were walking

My friend, Gill, and I (**1**) _____ our local running club (**2**) _____ fit. Gill (**3**) _____ some sport before, but I (**4**) _____ anything. To be honest, I (**5**) _____ a bit lazy! Anyway, last week, we (**6**) _____ _____ past the running track when we (**7**) _____ _____ some people training. It looked good fun, so we went in (**8**) _____ about joining. The coach was pleased because the club (**9**) _____ for new members. Our first training session is tomorrow, but I don't feel ready for it. I mean, I (**10**) _____ any trainers yet!

# Culture focus

**1** **Do the culture quiz. Look for the answers in your Student's Book and Workbook if necessary.**

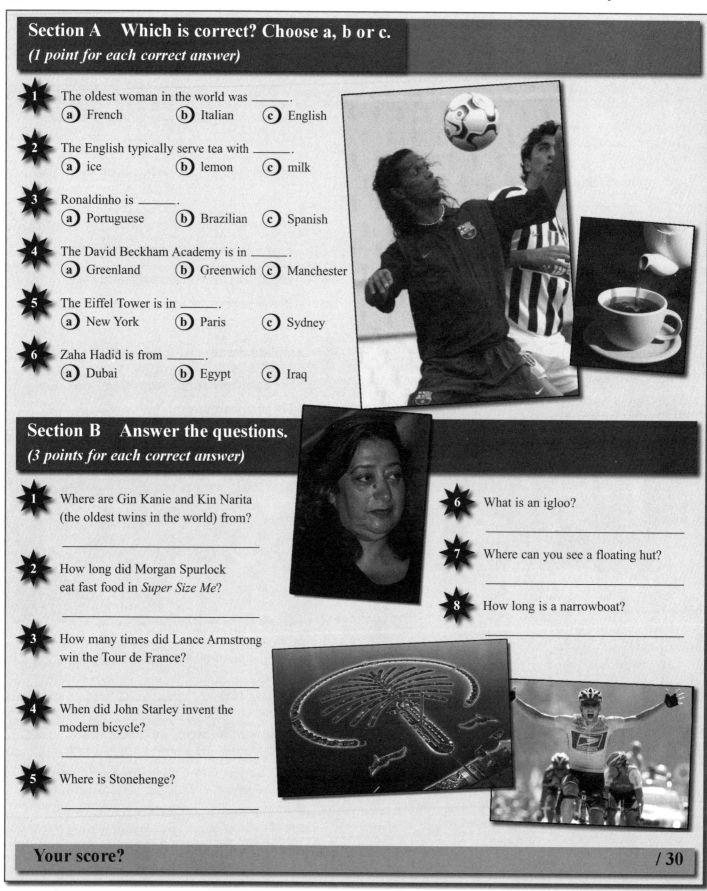

## Section A   Which is correct? Choose a, b or c.
*(1 point for each correct answer)*

**1** The oldest woman in the world was _____.
(a) French       (b) Italian       (c) English

**2** The English typically serve tea with _____.
(a) ice       (b) lemon       (c) milk

**3** Ronaldinho is _____.
(a) Portuguese       (b) Brazilian       (c) Spanish

**4** The David Beckham Academy is in _____.
(a) Greenland       (b) Greenwich       (c) Manchester

**5** The Eiffel Tower is in _____.
(a) New York       (b) Paris       (c) Sydney

**6** Zaha Hadid is from _____.
(a) Dubai       (b) Egypt       (c) Iraq

## Section B   Answer the questions.
*(3 points for each correct answer)*

**1** Where are Gin Kanie and Kin Narita (the oldest twins in the world) from?

_____

**2** How long did Morgan Spurlock eat fast food in *Super Size Me*?

_____

**3** How many times did Lance Armstrong win the Tour de France?

_____

**4** When did John Starley invent the modern bicycle?

_____

**5** Where is Stonehenge?

_____

**6** What is an igloo?

_____

**7** Where can you see a floating hut?

_____

**8** How long is a narrowboat?

_____

**Your score?**                                    **/ 30**

## Reading

### CANARIES TO THE CARIBBEAN

Cracknell and Fogle in *The Spirit of EDF Energy*

**A** James Cracknell, a British rower, is the winner of two Olympic gold medals. He feels rather worried when he thinks about the next two months, and he has good reason. At the weekend, he is flying to the Canary Islands to meet Ben Fogle, a British TV presenter. Together with 25 other teams, the two men are going to participate in the Atlantic Rowing Race. The problem is: Ben is not very experienced at rowing!

**B** Most of the teams have prepared for two years, but James and Ben have not. Until a few months ago, they did not even know each other, and James was thinking about rowing in the next Olympic Games, not rowing across the Atlantic. But then Ben made the suggestion after they met at a party.

**C** The 2,535-mile race is from La Gomera to Antigua. The two men are going to row 24 hours a day, taking it in turns to row for two hours and then rest for two hours. In 2003, two men from New Zealand broke the record for the race. They finished in 40 days, five hours and 31 minutes. Cracknell and Fogle are not going to beat that time, but they are planning to do it in 50 days.

**D** Cracknell and Fogle are not looking forward to the race, but they are determined to carry on until the end. They are not going to be completely alone in their seven-metre boat. There is a special camera in *The Spirit of EDF Energy*, and the BBC is going to make a programme about the race as soon as they complete it.

**1** Read the text quickly and choose the correct answer.

James Cracknell is going to (fly) / row to the Canary Islands.

1 Ben Fogle has / **has not** done a lot of rowing before.
2 It was **Cracknell's** / **Fogle's** idea to do the race.
3 Cracknell and Fogle are going to row their boat at **the same time** / **different times**.
4 Cracknell and Fogle **are** / **are not** faster rowers than the two New Zealanders.
5 They are **not** / **very** excited about the race.

**2** Answer the questions. Use full sentences.

Is James Cracknell experienced at rowing? How do you know?
Yes, he is. He has won two Olympic gold medals for rowing.

1 How many teams in total have entered the Atlantic Rowing Race?
_____

2 How are James Cracknell and Ben Fogle different from the other competitors?
_____
_____

3 How did Cracknell's plans change after he met Fogle?
_____
_____

4 What is the fastest that anybody has rowed across the Atlantic?
_____

5 What is unusual about their boat?
_____
_____

# Grammar

## Future forms (1): *going to*

**1** Complete the sentences with the *going to* form of the verbs in the box.

> you / do   give   give up   hurt   join   look up
> not take off   she / spend   ~~Pete / study~~

*Is Pete going to study* English at university?

1 My parents _____ smoking soon.
2 We _____ a sports club to make some friends.
3 Be careful! You _____ yourself.
4 It's freezing in here. I _____ my coat.
5 How much money _____ in town?
6 I _____ this new word.
7 Oh, no! The teacher _____ us another warning.
8 _____ karate today?

**2** Write with questions *going to*.

1 you / play / squash / tonight?
   *Are you going to play squash tonight?*
2 how / they / find / the answer?
   _____
   _____
3 your sister / go / to university?
   _____
   _____
4 you / speak / to Matthew / later?
   _____
   _____
5 it / be / cold / tomorrow?
   _____
   _____
6 Emma / use / the computer / now?
   _____
   _____

**3** Complete the answers with *going to*. Then match the answers with questions 1–6 in exercise 2.

a ☐ Yes, and I think it _____ (rain), too.
b ☐ 1 No, I'm *going to go* (go) jogging.
c ☐ No, I'm not. I _____ (send) him an email.
d ☐ They _____ (look) on the internet.
e ☐ No, she isn't. She _____ (get) a job.
f ☐ Yes, but she _____ (not be) a long time.

## Future forms (2): Present continuous

**4** Complete the sentences with the present continuous form of the verbs in the box.

> ~~fly~~   not get   you / go   not have
> they / look after   meet   participate

We're *flying* to Málaga at six o'clock.

1 They _____ each other outside the library at three o'clock.
2 _____ the children?
3 Natalie and Carl _____ married in June. The wedding is in July.
4 Thousands of people _____ in the race on Sunday.
5 Sara _____ a picnic tomorrow. It's on Friday.
6 _____ skiing this winter?

**5** Read the diary. Then write sentences about Katy's arrangements. Use the affirmative or negative form of the present continuous.

| | |
|---|---|
| **Monday 21** | meet Lisa in the internet café |
| **Tuesday 22** | **(1)** watch DVDs at Mark's house |
| **Wednesday 23** | **(2)** play volleyball after school |
| **Thursday 24** | **(3)** ~~have piano lesson~~ |
| **Friday 25** | **(4)** travel to Oxford |
| **Saturday 26** | **(5)** spend the weekend with Aunty May |
| **Sunday 27** | ↓ |

Katy is meeting Lisa in the internet café on Monday.

1 She _____

_____

2 _____

_____

3 _____

_____

4 _____

_____

5 _____

_____

# Future time expressions

**6** Match 1–6 with a–f. Then complete the sentences with the correct form of the verb in brackets.

1 [c] We're going shopping ...
2 [ ] Billy and I are going to phone as ...
3 [ ] My mum is going to be home by ...
4 [ ] Tony's going to be famous ...
5 [ ] He's going to stay in bed ...
6 [ ] She's going to look for some shoes ...

a after he _____ (appear) on TV.
b while she _____ (be) in London.
c when we stay (stay) in London.
d the time we _____ (get) there.
e until he _____ (feel) better.
f soon as we _____ (hear) the news.

## Consolidation

**7** Complete the dialogue. Use the *going to* (GT) or present continuous (PC) form of the verbs in the box.

do    watch    run    get    go    ~~you / do~~
not wear    not be    you / win

Sam    I'm worried about the weekend.
Lee    Why? What are you doing (PC)?
Sam    I **(1)** _____ (PC) in the London Marathon on Sunday.
Lee    Really? Is it difficult? **(2)** _____ _____ (GT)?
Sam    No, I don't think so! I **(3)** _____ (PC) it with my friend from Birmingham, but we **(4)** _____ (GT) shorts and T-shirts. We've got costumes: we **(5)** _____ (GT) as sunflowers!
Lee    Flowers? That **(6)** _____ _____ (GT) easy, is it?
Sam    No, it isn't, and we **(7)** _____ _____ (GT) really hot, too.
Lee    Well, good luck! I wasn't going to do anything special on Sunday, but now I **(8)** _____ (GT) the marathon on TV and look for you!

# Communication

## Vocabulary Phrasal verbs (1)

**1** Complete the crossword.

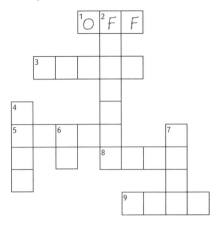

### Across (→)

1 to remove (some clothes) = to take *off*
3 to continue (something) = to _____ on
5 to care for (somebody / something) = to look _____
8 to think that you are better than (somebody) = to look _____ on
9 to find a word (in a dictionary) = to _____ up

### Down (↓)

2 to wait with pleasure (for something) = to look _____ to
4 to return (somewhere) = to go _____
6 to admire (somebody) = to look up _____
7 to investigate (something) = to look _____

**2** Complete the sentences with phrasal verbs from exercise 1.

You mustn't *look down on* other people.
1 I'm tired. Let's _____ home.
2 Here's my new digital camera. Remember: please _____ it!
3 _____ those boots! They're really dirty.
4 Do you always _____ your holidays?
5 Don't stop reading! _____!

## get

**3** Match the bold verbs in sentences 1–7 with the meanings a–g.

1 [c] Mark **got** a job after he left school.
2 [ ] I **got** some new jeans today.
3 [ ] Is Ella going to **get** better?
4 [ ] What time do you **get to** school?
5 [ ] We didn't have coats, so we **got** cold.
6 [ ] You've just **got** a text message.
7 [ ] They **got** home late last night.

a become          e arrived
b received         f became
c obtained         g bought
d arrive at

## Speaking Plans to meet

**4** Complete the dialogue with the words in the box.

then   time   forward   fancy   ~~week~~   about
while   morning   soon

Mary    I'm going to Paris with my mum next *week*. I'm really looking (1) _____ to it!

Beth    Lucky you! I'm still at school on Monday (2) _____.

Mary    I know. By the (3) _____ you finish school at three o'clock, I'm going to be in France!

Beth    What are you going to do (4) _____ you're there?

Mary    Shopping! We're going to go shopping as (5) _____ as we arrive!

Beth    Do you (6) _____ meeting for a coffee on Sunday?

Mary    I'd love to. How (7) _____ JoJo's at eleven?

Beth    Great. See you (8) _____.

# Writing

## An informal letter  Parts of a letter

**1** Complete the letter with the words in the box.

> ~~Croft~~  Emma  ~~11~~  Write  July  Manchester  Grandma and Grandpa  16th  Love  Dear  soon  Road

11 Croft **(1)** _____

**(2)** _____

**(3)** _____ _____

**(4)** _____ _____

Sorry I haven't written for a long time, but I've been really busy recently. I've had a lot of school work to do. We're taking exams at the beginning of March and I haven't had any free time at weekends, either.

This weekend, I'm playing in a hockey match on Saturday morning. We lost our last two matches, but I'm sure we're going to win this one because we've practised a lot!

In the afternoon, I'm going back home to get changed and then I'm meeting some friends from my old school at my favourite café in town. I can't wait!

**(5)** _____ _____ ,

**(6)** _____

**(7)** _____

me – playing hockey last week

**2** Write the last paragraph of Emma's letter. Put the words in the correct order.

Mum and Dad / Last week, / Guess what? / our holiday. / organised

1 in May. / trekking and horse riding / going / in the mountains / We're

2 It's / be / going to / brilliant!

3 We / Mum / camping / outdoors! / aren't going / like sleeping / because / doesn't

Guess what? Last week, Mum and Dad organised our holiday. _____
_____
_____
_____

# Quick check

## Vocabulary

**1** Complete the sentences with the phrasal verbs in the box.

> carry on   go back   look after   look forward to
> look up   look into

1 I'm staying at home to _____ my sister.
2 The head teacher is going to _____ the problems at our school.
3 Clare left school last year, but now she wants to _____ .
4 Rafa loves studying English. He's decided to _____ learning it next year.
5 Why don't you _____ those words in your dictionary?
6 I never _____ exams.

**2** Choose the correct meaning of *get*.

1 Julie's getting worried about her exams. (obtain / become)
2 When did you get home? (receive / arrive)
3 Where can I get a DVD? (obtain / receive)
4 We got to school early today. (arrive / obtain)
5 My grandpa's memory is getting worse. (become / arrive)
6 I didn't get your message. (arrive / receive)

## Vocabulary review: Units 1–4

**3** Choose the correct answer.

Billy Weaver has a dream: to (1) **play / do** football for England. He's the captain of our school team. He's good at giving (2) **suggestions / advice** and he's also very (3) **sensitive / insensitive** – you can discuss anything with him.
Billy loves football. He (4) **takes off / puts on** his boots after school and spends hours and hours on the (5) **pitch / court**.
All the players (6) **look forward to / look up to** him. He has taught us never to (7) **carry on / give up**.
I really hope he (8) **becomes / gets** a place in the England football team.

## Grammar

**4** Complete the sentences with the *going to* form of the verbs in the box.

> she / get   not eat   not speak   win
> you / watch

1 Look! Kim _____ the race.
2 We _____ in that restaurant again. It was terrible.
3 When _____ married?
4 Gary is so rude. I _____ to him again.
5 _____ that film tonight?

**5** Write the sentences. Use the present continuous form of the verbs.

1 you / do / anything / this weekend / ?
_____
2 we / give / concert / on Saturday
_____
3 she / not go / on tour / next year
_____
4 they / prepare / for their exams / tomorrow / ?
_____

## Grammar review: Units 1–4

**6** Choose the correct answer.

I'm looking forward to summer this year because I (1) **'ve worked / 'm working** in America in July. I (2) **read / was reading** a friend's magazine last month when I (3) **saw / was seeing** the job advert. The company (4) **looked for / was looking for** adventurous eighteen-year-olds who enjoy sport, so I decided (5) **am applying / to apply**. Although I've (6) **never / ever** done anything like this before, ¡ (7) **didn't get / got** the job!

(8) **As soon as / By the time** school finishes, I'm meeting everybody in Florida. I've never been away from home (9) **since / for** more than two weeks! We (10) **were having / 're going to have** a great time.

## Reading

### HAVE YOU BLOGGED TODAY?

SEARCH THIS BLOG   START YOUR OWN BLOG   NEXT BLOG

**A** Most people use the internet as soon as there is something they want to find out. Whether it is information for homework or the times of films at the cinema, the internet has become our first point of reference. It is like having all the world's libraries at your fingertips.

**B** When you look at the internet, you'll see 'blogs' everywhere, but what exactly is a blog? The word 'blog' is very new, so it is not in many dictionaries yet. It is a noun and a regular verb. It comes from 'weblog'. 'Web' means 'internet' and 'log' means 'diary', so 'blog' means 'internet diary'.

**C** There are millions of blogs on the web. They can be about absolutely anything, but they are often about personal opinions or experiences, like a diary. The 'blogger', or writer, is like a newspaper columnist, but without any special training. Anybody can write a blog – and everybody can read it!

**D** Blogs first appeared in the late 1990s, but there has been an enormous increase in their popularity since 2000. Nowadays, everybody has their own blog: politicians, singers, scientists, artists, policemen, teachers and, of course, students and schoolchildren, are writing blogs. Blogs are becoming the fastest way that news circulates.

**E** Blogs are a part of modern life and they are here to stay. So, if there is something you would like to tell the world, why not start writing? Creating your own blog is incredibly easy, so start up your computer and blog!

**ABOUT ME**

Name:
Georgia Bushell

View my profile

**PREVIOUS POSTS**

Hi! Welcome to my blog

**ARCHIVES**

**1** **Read the text. Match the headings 1–6 with paragraphs A–E. (There is one heading you do not need.)**

1 ☐ What is a blog?   4 ☐ Bloggers at home
2 ☐ Start blogging!   5 ☐A A useful resource
3 ☐ Who is blogging?  6 ☐ Express yourself

**2** **Answer the questions. Use full sentences.**

Where do most people look for information?
*Most people look for information on the internet.*

1 What is the origin of the word 'blog'?
_____

2 What type of writing is similar to a blog?
_____

3 What limits are there on writing and reading blogs?
_____

4 In which century did blogs become really popular?
_____

5 Who blogs?
_____

# Grammar

## Future forms (3): *will*

**1** **Write the sentences.**

look up / the dictionary / They / in / 'll / the word
*They'll look up the word in the dictionary.*

1  next / the / Italy / win / World Cup / Will / ?

　_____

2  Will / your brother / a teacher / be / ?

　_____

3  anything, / We / eat / won't / thanks

　_____

4  I / an email / 'll / every day / send / Kate

　_____

5  like / You / that film / won't

　_____

6  next / read / you / Which / book / will / ?

　_____

**2** **Complete the sentences with *will* / *'ll* or *won't*
and the verbs in the box.**

> become  go back  forget  have  open  ~~snow~~
> tell  understand  write

It*'ll snow* tomorrow.

1  Remember that John doesn't speak French. He
　_____ anything.

2  I _____ to you every day, I
　promise!

3  My sister doesn't know what job she wants, but
　she _____ a doctor. She hates
　hospitals!

4  'It's very hot in here.'
　'I _____ the window for you.'

5  We know it's a secret, so don't worry! We
　_____ anybody.

6  'Would you like a drink?'
　'I _____ a coffee, please.'

7  The library was closed. I _____
　tomorrow.

8  Don't worry. We _____ mum's
　birthday present this time!

**3** **What are the people saying? Write sentences
with the expressions in the box and *'ll* or *won't*.**

> she / not speak / to you　　he / not enjoy / it
> ~~I / open / the door~~　　I / study / more

I'll open the door.

1  _____

2  _____

3  _____

# First conditional

**4** Match 1–6 with a–f. Then complete the sentences with the correct form of the verbs.

1 [b] If you look up the word, …
2 [ ] Peter won't pass his exams …
3 [ ] If Lindsay practises more, …
4 [ ] She won't have any more money …
5 [ ] He'll send you an email …
6 [ ] Sue will take lots of photos …

a if she _____ (buy) that MP3 player.
b you'll find out (find out) its meaning.
c her Arabic _____ (improve).
d if she _____ (borrow) your camera.
e if he _____ (not work) harder.
f if he _____ (log on).

**5** Write the sentences. Use the first conditional form of the verbs. Add a comma (,) if necessary.

if / I / put on / the goggles / I / look / silly
If I put on the goggles, I'll look silly.

1 if / Tom / see / that film / he / get / scared

_____

_____

2 your brother / help / us / if / we / ask / him / ?

_____

_____

3 Ms Ross / not be / happy / if / you / arrive / late

_____

_____

4 if / I / send / an email / you / reply / soon / ?

_____

_____

## *if* or *when*?

**6** Complete the sentences with *if* or *when*.

Don't look! If you look, you'll see your present.

1 I don't usually see Howard. _____ I see him tomorrow, I'll say hello.
2 Jenny hasn't arrived yet. We'll tell you _____ she gets here.
3 Tom is unfriendly. He never smiles _____ I see him every morning.
4 We won't go to the beach _____ it rains.

# Consolidation

**7** Correct the mistake in each sentence.

We buy a new printer if we'll have enough money.
*We'll buy a new printer if we have enough money.*

1 I not say anything, I promise.

_____

2 This exercise is very hard, but I will give up.

_____

3 We'll feel miserable when nobody comes to the match.

_____

4 If it'll be sunny tomorrow, Greg and I will play tennis.

_____

5 'My bag is heavy.' 'I carry it for you!'

_____

6 Jake plays music all the time. I hate it if he does that.

_____

**8** Complete the text with the words in the box.

'll find   ~~'ll hear~~   If   vote   when   will play
won't believe   won't get

## TeenTunes ♪♫

TeenTunes is *the* radio station for cool teenagers. If you tune in, you'll hear all the latest hits. And it's interactive, too! You (1) _____ a list of songs (2) _____ you log on to the TeenTunes website. If you (3) _____ for your favourite songs, then James Matthews (4) _____ them on his show.

You (5) _____ TeenTunes if you've got an old-fashioned radio – it has to be a DAB digital radio. So, enter TeenTunes's competition and win a new DAB digital radio! (6) _____ you are one of the ten lucky winners, you (7) _____ the amazing sound quality of DAB! Hurry and enter now.

# Communication

## Vocabulary   Digital technology

**1** Complete the labels.

c a b l e s

1 _ _ g _ _ _ l   c _ _ _ r _

2 _ e _ _ o _ _ d

3 s _ _ _ k _ _ s

4 _ _ _ s _

5 m _ _ i _ _ r

6 _ _ 3 _ l _ _ _ r

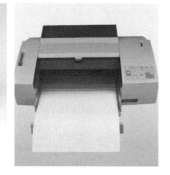

7 p _ _ n _ _ r

## Phrasal verbs (2)

**2** Match 1–6 with a–f to complete the definitions.

1 [ b ]  You shut down the computer …
2 [ ]  You tune in a radio …
3 [ ]  You turn up the TV …
4 [ ]  To start up your computer, …
5 [ ]  You plug in a laptop …
6 [ ]  You turn over the TV …

a   to hear it better.
b   to turn it off.
c   to change channels.
d   to find a radio station.
e   you press the 'On' button.
f   to recharge the battery.

## Speaking   A digital radio

**3** Complete the dialogue with the words in the box. Then choose the correct answer for a–d.

> Finally   First   Next   Then

**Grandpa**  I've just bought a digital **mouse** / (radio), but I don't know how it works.

**Simon**  I'll show you. **(1)** ——————, decide where to (a) **log on** / **plug in** the radio.

**Grandpa**  OK. I'll put it here.

**Simon**  **(2)** ——————, find the 'On' button. When you press that, it (b) **turns on** / **shuts down** the radio.
**(3)** ——————, if you press this button, the names of the radio stations appear on that small (c) **screen** / **speaker**. Press the button until you find the station that you want.

**Grandpa**  That's very easy, isn't it?

**Simon**  Yes, it is, and if you press the red button, it (d) **tunes in** / **turns up** the volume. **(4)** ——————, just sit back and enjoy the programme!

**Grandpa**  I will! Thanks very much.

# Writing

## Instant messaging   Colloquial expressions

**1** Put the parts of an instant message dialogue a–j in order 1–10.

a ☐ Yeah. I really like ur mob. If I've got enough money, I'll get 1 like that. 🎁

b ☐ I was talking 2 John when I dropped it in the bath! 😳

c ☐ Dunno. When is his bday? 🤔

d ☐ Why's it broken? Wot happened? 🤔

e ☑ 10  Yes! See u there. Bye! 😃

f ☐ 1  R u going 2 go out 4 Raj's bday? 🤔

g ☐ No way! 😳 R u going 2 get a new 1? 🤔

h ☐ Good idea! 😃 See u at 8 on Raj's bday!

i ☐ I didn't get 1. My mob's broken.

j ☐ On Saturday. He sent a text 2 ur mob yesterday.

*[window buttons: Join a chat | New | Exit]*

**2** Write the dialogue in exercise 1 in the correct order. Change the short forms into full forms.

1 Are you going to go out for Raj's birthday?
2 _____
3 _____
4 _____
5 _____
6 _____
7 _____
8 _____
9 _____
10 Yes! See you there! Bye!

**3** Write the instant messages using short forms.

Can I go to your birthday party?
Can I go 2 ur bday party?

1 What are you doing for your birthday?

_____

2 Are you going to town to look for a new mobile?

_____

3 I don't know. What are you going to do?

_____

4 I can give you one for your birthday.

_____

5 See you on your birthday.

_____

# Quick check

## Vocabulary

**1 Choose the correct digital technology word.**

1 There's a button on each **printer / speaker** to change the volume.
2 How many songs are there on your **digital camera / MP3 player**?
3 I hate typing on this **keyboard / cable**.
4 The **monitor / mouse** doesn't work. Martin clicked on 'Exit', but nothing happened.
5 I can't plug in the **screen / computer**. The cable isn't long enough.

**2 Complete the sentences with the phrasal verbs in the box.**

| log on   plug in   start up   tune in   turn off |
| --- |

1 Don't _____ the TV here.
2 It's easy to _____ to stations with digital radios.
3 Please _____ the music. It's time for bed.
4 Press this to _____ the computer.
5 You need to _____ to the internet.

## Vocabulary review: Units 1–5

**3 Choose the correct answer.**

Last June, I was online when I found an amazing (1) **digital camera / website**. It was about winter sports, such as (2) **windsurfing / snowboarding**.

I decided to try snowboarding, and I've been several times now. I love it, although I'm still very (3) **inexperienced / unmotivated** and I fall over a lot. Snowboarders definitely need to be (4) **patient / impatient**. If you aren't, you'll (5) **look up / give up** very quickly. You don't need much equipment, just a board and some (6) **poles / goggles**. However, if you want to look (7) **cool / sympathetic**, you'll have to (8) **get / become** the right clothes.

## Grammar

**4 Complete the sentences with your opinion. Use will / 'll or won't.**

1 People _____ (use) instant messaging in the future.
2 It _____ (rain) tomorrow.
3 My parents _____ (develop) a computer program this year.
4 I _____ (live) in Paris.
5 I _____ (get) 15 emails today.

**5 Complete the sentences. Use the first conditional form of the verbs in brackets.**

1 If he _____ (press) that button, the computer _____ (start up).
2 They _____ (get) angry if you _____ (not turn over) the TV.
3 I _____ (reply) when I _____ (get) your email.
4 When we _____ (log on), we _____ (visit) the school website.
5 What _____ (you / say) if he _____ (break) the camera?

## Grammar review: Units 1–5

**6 Choose the correct answer.**

Dear Carla

We're on holiday in Lisbon! We (1) **haven't visited / weren't visiting** Portugal before, so it's very exciting.
We've (2) **just / yet** been to the Museum of Telecommunications to see a 'house of the future'.
The house is completely interactive, so if you (3) **'ll press / press** buttons on the phone, the doors (4) **will open / are opening** or the coffee machine (5) **will / won't** turn on! We'll tell you more about it (6) **if / when** we see you next month.
We (7) **'re going to spend / 've spent** two more days in Lisbon and then we're going to Coimbra.
We'll phone you as soon as we (8) **'re getting / get** home.

Love Kath and Julie xxxx

# 6 | Habits and homes

## Reading

**Joe** Have you seen this amazing bedroom? It's in a new hotel in the Bahamas called The Poseidon Resort, and it's 20 metres underwater! Imagine lying in that bed. All the fish would swim over you, but you wouldn't get wet!

**Lisa** It looks incredible. I'd love to stay there.

**Joe** Well, it isn't opening until next year, but you'll need to save a lot of money because it'll be really expensive. Actually, I wouldn't want to sleep there. I'd feel a little nervous if I was underwater all night. I'd rather stay in an ice hotel.

**Lisa** There aren't hotels made of ice, are there?

**Joe** There are a few! I've read about one in Sweden. It's 120 km from the North Pole and it's completely made of ice. The drinks come in an ice glass, the dinner is on an ice plate, you sit on an ice chair – you even sleep on an ice bed!

**Lisa** That's sounds terrible. I'd be freezing if I stayed there!

**Joe** Well, maybe you'd like a place called Guadix, in Spain. They build their homes underground to escape the summer heat. Apparently, almost half of Guadix's inhabitants live underground in cave houses. Last year, some of my friends stayed in a cave hotel there.

**Lisa** I bet the houses are cold in winter, aren't they?

**Joe** No, it's strange, but the thick walls make the temperature inside about 19°C all year. My friends looked in one of the houses and it was just like any other Spanish home – marble floors and comfortable furniture – and this cave even had the internet!

**1** **Read the text quickly and choose the correct answer.**

Joe / (Lisa) wants to stay at The Poseidon Resort.
1 The Poseidon Resort **will** / **won't** be very cheap.
2 Lisa **knows a lot** / **doesn't know** about ice hotels.
3 **More** / **Less** than 50% of Guadix's population lives in a cave.
4 Joe **has** / **hasn't** visited Guadix.
5 People in Guadix live in caves to **keep** / **look** cool.

**2** **Answer the questions. Use full sentences.**

What is unusual about The Poseidon Resort?
*It is 20 metres underwater.*

1 Why would Joe not stay at The Poseidon Resort?

_____

_____

2 What is the furniture like in the ice hotel?

_____

3 Are the Guadix caves warmer in winter or summer? Why?

_____

_____

4 Was the Guadix cave house very different from a Spanish house? Why? / Why not?

_____

_____

# Grammar

## Second conditional

**1** Complete the dialogue with the phrases in the box.

would annoy  'd be  'd miss  listened  slept
did  ~~wouldn't like~~  wouldn't tidy  wouldn't sleep

**Sophie** This is my bed and that's Clare's. She's my sister.

**Leah** I *wouldn't like* it if I shared a room with my sister, Jane.

**Sophie** Why not? It isn't that bad.

**Leah** You should see Jane's room! It's so untidy. She (1) _____ the room if she shared with me. And the wardrobe would be full of her clothes.

**Sophie** I (2) _____ Clare if she had her own bedroom. Sometimes she's annoying, but we love chatting. It (3) _____ very quiet if she wasn't there.

**Leah** Well, Jane wouldn't talk to me if she (4) _____ in my room. She'd listen to her stereo all the time. I don't like her music, so it (5) _____ me if we shared.

**Sophie** But if she (6) _____ to music on an MP3 player, you wouldn't hear it, would you?

**Leah** I suppose not. Anyway, I (7) _____ if Jane had a bed near me.

**Sophie** Why not?

**Leah** She shouts at night. I'd never sleep if she (8) _____ that!

**2** Put the words in the correct order. Add commas (,) if necessary.

went / If / visit / we / England / we'd / on holiday
*If we went on holiday, we'd visit England.*

1 spoke / you / wouldn't / if / They / in German / understand / you

_____

2 if / moved house / have / a bigger room / I'd / we

_____

3 won / you / the big prize / you / If / do / what / would / ?

_____

4 Carl / If / left / he / a job / school / get / wouldn't

_____

5 shy / you / Would / you / feel / met / if / a famous person / ?

_____

6 If / on the internet / you / you / 'd / find / the answer / looked

_____

**3** Match 1–7 with a–g. Then complete the sentences with the correct form of the verbs in brackets.

1 [c] If we supported a famous team, ...
2 [ ] His English would get better ...
3 [ ] If I had a computer, ...
4 [ ] If you gave me a heavy metal CD, ...
5 [ ] I'd take a lot of photos ...
6 [ ] Our parents would be pleased ...
7 [ ] I'd get upset ...

a I _____ (not listen) to it!
b if I _____ (have) a digital camera.
c we'd *watch* (watch) them every week.
d if I _____ (lose) £20.
e if he _____ (practise) more.
f if we _____ (go) to university.
g I _____ (use) it every day.

**4** Complete the sentences. Use the second conditional form of the verbs in brackets.

If Amir _knew_ (know) the answer, he _'d tell_ (tell) you.

1 They _____ (enjoy) the film if they _____ (see) it.
2 If I _____ (read) that book, it _____ (take) a long time.
3 _____ (Lisa / feel) scared if she _____ (go) on a plane?
4 I _____ (not stay) in a cave hotel if I _____ (visit) Guadix.
5 If you _____ (cycle) to school, you _____ (get) there sooner.
6 We _____ (do) more exercise if we _____ (have) more time.

# Quantifiers

**5** Complete the dialogue with the words in the box.

> a few   a few   a little   A lot of   any   many
> ~~much~~   much

Anna    That looks like a good book. Are you enjoying it?

Ben    I'm only on page 45, so I haven't read _much_, but it's really exciting.

Anna    I haven't read (1) _____ good books recently – not one.
(2) _____ books are interesting at the start, but then I get bored after only (3) _____ chapters.

Ben    Why not read (4) _____ of this now? If you like it, I'll lend it to you in (5) _____ days.

Anna    Really? How (6) _____ books do you read every week?

Ben    It depends. I try to read as (7) _____ as possible.

**6** Correct the mistake in each sentence.

Hurry up! We haven't got many time.
_Hurry up! We haven't got much time._

1 Crisps? Oh, yes, please. Just a little.

_____

2 I haven't got many homework. It'll only take ten minutes.

_____

_____

3 He's spent everything. He hasn't got much money now.

_____

_____

4 We've got a few food in the fridge.

_____

5 That's too many! I only like a little milk in coffee.

_____

_____

6 There are lot of books on the shelves.

_____

# Consolidation

**7** Complete the text with the words in the box.

> A few   'd want   downloaded   wanted   many
> much   some   ~~was~~   would increase

If I _was_ a singer and I (1) _____ to get to number 1 in the UK pop music charts, I (2) _____ a lot of people to download my record from the internet.
(3) _____ years ago, not (4) _____ people did this, but a recent survey has revealed that the British are the biggest downloaders in Europe. They don't spend (5) _____ (about 75p a month), but they downloaded more than 23 million songs last year, a 400% increase on the previous year.
In the survey, (6) _____ people admitted using illegal websites to download free music. If everybody (7) _____ music legally, sales (8) _____ even more.

# Communication

## Vocabulary Household nouns

**1** Label the objects in the picture.

| | |
|---|---|
| 1 | shelf |
| 2 | b _____ |
| 3 | a _____ |
| 4 | s _____ |
| 5 | d _____ |
| 6 | w _____ |
| | m _____ |
| 7 | c _____ |
| 8 | c _____ |
| 9 | s _____ |
| 10 | f _____ |

### *have* and *make*

**2** Complete the sentences with *have* or *make*.

This is tiring. Let's *have* a rest!

1 Why do you always _____ such a mess?
2 Do you usually _____ a laugh at the youth club?
3 Shhh! I'm going to _____ an important phone call.
4 Did you _____ fun last night?
5 I always _____ an effort.
6 If we _____ a problem, I'll call you.
7 Some people _____ excuses about everything.
8 Let's _____ lunch. I'm hungry!

## Speaking A football match

**3** Write the sentences in the correct order.

Lisa  town / fancy / Do / on / you / Saturday / to / afternoon? / coming
(1) _____
_____

Sarah  match. / I'm / but / football / going / a / Sorry, / to
(2) _____
_____

Lisa  going / Really? / you / to / matches? / Do / like
(3) _____
_____

Sarah  shouting / for / Yes, / love / team! / I / my
(4) _____
_____

any / ever / go / you / to / Do / matches?
(5) _____
_____

Lisa  sport / watching / TV. / prefer / I / on / No,
(6) _____
_____

the / I / like / in / standing / outside / cold! / don't
(7) _____
_____

# Writing

## A lifestyle description  Modifiers

**1  Complete the sentences with the correct word.**

Our house is *not particularly* big, but it's very comfortable. (**extremely / not particularly**)

1  That DVD was _____ amazing. I'd love to see it again. (**not at all / really**)

2  This room is _____ big. There isn't much space for furniture. (**not particularly / really**)

3  The book is _____ interesting, but I wouldn't recommend it. (**quite / not at all**)

4  Although maths is _____ interesting, I'm going to carry on studying it. (**not at all / extremely**)

5  If I failed all my exams, my parents would be _____ angry. (**not at all / really**)

6  Alice is very outgoing. She is _____ shy. (**quite / not at all**)

7  It was _____ cold yesterday. It was –5°C all day. (**extremely / quite**)

**2  Read the descriptions. Then label them with the words in the box. (There is one word you do not need.)**

bedroom   dining room   garden   kitchen living room

**A** _____

This is my least favourite room in our house. It isn't particularly large, but there's an enormous table in it. It's always freezing in this room, so we don't use it very often – everybody prefers eating somewhere warmer!

**B** _____

We've just painted this room, so it's really nice now. We've got an armchair and an extremely comfortable sofa. The sofa is quite useful because it becomes a bed – my friends visit me quite a lot, and they sleep on it when they visit. There isn't a TV in here because my parents don't like watching TV in the evenings.

**C** _____

I love this place. It's quite long and it's really warm and sunny, especially in summer. My friends and I play football here all the time. There isn't much furniture – just a wooden bench under a beautiful old tree. The cat really enjoys sitting there!

**D** _____

This room isn't particularly big, but it's where I spend 90% of my time. There's a small chest of drawers in the corner with a portable TV on it. I love watching films in bed. There isn't any space for a wardrobe – I have to share my sister's.

**3  Look at the photo. Then complete the description with the phrases in the box.**

quite modern   not particularly old   quite rich
extremely light   really large   at all comfortable

This bedroom is (1) _____, about 35m². It's (2) _____ because there are a lot of windows. There isn't much furniture and it's all (3) _____. The room doesn't look (4) _____! The people who own this room like reading and relaxing. They're probably (5) _____ and (6) _____.

## Vocabulary

**1** Complete the sentences with the correct household noun.

1 If we had some b_____, we could put all our books on them.
2 Put the dirty plates in the s_____. I'll do the washing up later.
3 I haven't got a d_____ in my room, so I do my homework on the kitchen table.
4 The cups are in the c_____ next to the fridge.
5 My sister keeps old letters in a b_____ at the top of her wardrobe.

**2** Choose the correct answer.

1 Has Tom **had** / **made** a mess again?
2 Don't **make** / **have** excuses!
3 I hate **making** / **having** problems.
4 Did you **make** / **have** a laugh?
5 They never **have** / **make** an effort.

## Vocabulary review: Units 1–6

**3** Complete the text with the words in the box.

> computer   dining table   getting   hard-working
> rest   screen   turning on   unmotivated   warning
> washing machine

A lot of people work at home these days.
You don't even need a desk – you can put your
(1) _____ on the (2) _____.
If you're (3) _____, you'll probably work
longer hours than in an office, because you won't
waste time going to work and (4) _____
home. However, let me give you a (5) _____
for when you are an adult about to start working: if
you're lazy and (6) _____, you won't get up
in the mornings. And if you're bored of looking at the
computer (7) _____, you'll find a lot of
other things to do – putting the dirty clothes in the
(8) _____, doing the
cleaning, or even having a (9)_____ and
(10) _____ the TV!

## Grammar

**4** Complete the sentences. Use the second conditional form of the verbs in brackets.

1 If I _____ (see) Ronaldinho, I _____ (ask) for his autograph.
2 It _____ (be) really incredible if it _____ (snow) in August.
3 What _____ (your dad / do) if he _____ (give up) work?
4 My mum _____ (buy) a dishwasher if she _____ (have) enough money.
5 If we _____ (read) more books, _____ (we / learn) more vocabulary?
6 If we _____ (live) in a bigger flat, I _____ (not share) a room with my brother.

**5** Complete the sentences with the quantifiers in the box.

> a few   any   a little   a lot of   many

1 There isn't _____ money. Not one penny!
2 'Would you like some water?'
   'Just _____. I'm not very thirsty.'
3 Sue has got _____ CDs – hundreds!
4 There weren't _____ people at the meeting. I only knew two people.
5 We need more apples. We've only got _____.

## Grammar review: Units 1–6

**6** Choose the correct answer.

**Pete**     Do you know where Room 5 is?
**Teacher**  Yes, I (1) **'m going** / **'m not going** there in a moment. I (2) **show** / **'ll show** the way. If you (3) **waited** / **wait** here, I'll take you in a minute … (4) **You have** / **Have you** joined the school recently?
**Pete**     Yes, I've (5) **just** / **already** started and I (6) **got** / **was getting** very lost this morning! I (7) **looked** / **was looking** for the computer room when I (8) **found** / **was finding** myself in a cookery class!
**Teacher**  Really? Hurry up! Ms Palmer (9) **gets** / **got** angry if people (10) **are** / **be** late.

# Revision: Units 4-6

## Vocabulary

**1** Complete the puzzle. What is the mystery household noun?

The mystery household noun is _____.

1 You look at the _____ on your computer.
2 You click and move things on your computer with a _____.
3 You listen to music through a _____.
4 You can keep things in a _____.
5 You use a _____ to type on your computer.
6 You sit on an _____ in the living room.
7 You keep food cold in the _____.
8 You keep clothes in a _____ _____ _____.

**2** Complete the sentences with the prepositions in the box.

> down  in  into  off  on  over  to  up

1 When are you going to give _____ smoking?
2 I don't look _____ on anybody.
3 The school is looking _____ the problem of students copying homework from the internet.
4 She was tired, but she carried _____.
5 Log _____ the internet before you shut down the computer.
6 This programme is boring. Can I turn _____?
7 I plugged _____ the printer, but it didn't work.
8 I really look up _____ my parents. They're great.

**3** Complete the sentences with *get*, *have* or *make*.

1 If we _____ a mess, my mum and dad will _____ angry with me.
2 If the baby doesn't _____ a rest, he'll cry and _____ a lot of noise.
3 'We're going to _____ a laugh at the picnic.' 'Yes, you'll _____ fun!'
4 I must _____ a phone call because I'm going to _____ home late tonight.

**4** Complete the text with the words in the box.

> computer  furniture  get  log  put
> speaker  turn  website

### Crazy inventions!

Next time you're online, (**1**) _____ on to crazyinventions.com. It's such a fantastic (**2**) _____! They've got an amazing wardrobe – and it isn't just for your clothes. It looks like a normal piece of (**3**) _____, but it's electronic. When you (**4**) _____ on the wardobe in the morning, the (**5**) _____ inside it will (**6**) _____ information about the weather from the internet. Then a (**7**) _____ tells you what the weather is going to be like and the wardrobe chooses the best clothes for you to (**8**) _____ on!

# Grammar

**1** Complete the interview. Use the *going to* form of the verbs in brackets.

**Reporter** Well done! _____
(**1** you / make) any changes to the team?

**Captain** Definitely not. We _____
_____ (**2** carry on) training as usual and we _____
_____ (**3** get) even better!

**Reporter** What _____
(**4** you / do) with the money you've won?

**Captain** The manager _____
(**5** buy) new boots for the whole team.

**Reporter** You're all taking an important exam on Monday. _____
_____ (**6** you / revise) for the rest of the weekend?

**Captain** No, we _____
(**7** not worry) about that. We _____ _____ (**8** enjoy) the moment!

**2** Complete the sentences. Use the present continuous form of the verbs in the box.

fly   discuss   not go   you / meet   stay

1 What time _____ James tonight?
2 They _____ the problem at the meeting tomorrow.
3 Emma _____ at Anna's house on Saturday night.
4 We _____ on tour next summer. We haven't got time.
5 I'm so excited. I _____ to New York next week.

**3** Complete the sentences with the correct time expression.

1 It'll be dark _____ we get home. (**while / by the time**)
2 The computer won't work _____ you plug it in! (**after / until**)
3 _____ it is nine o'clock, lessons begin. (**As soon as / While**)
4 Leo will have a great time _____ he's in Cairo. (**by the time / while**)
5 My parents will be pleased _____ they get my exam results. (**when / until**)
6 Elsa is going to look for a flat _____ she arrives in London. (**after / while**)

**4** Complete the text with the words in the box.

drop   'll enjoy   'll log off   'll explain   'll win
~~log on~~   serve   'll speak   won't get

## Waiter!

I'm playing my favourite online game at the moment. If you log on to funnygames.com, you'll find it. It's called 'Waiter!'.
I (**1**) _____ how to play the game.

You are working in a café. A lot of people come in and sit down. You take their orders. They (**2**) _____ quickly, so listen carefully! If you (**3**) _____ the wrong food or drinks to people, then you'll lose points. You'll also lose points if you (**4**) _____ things! However, you (**5**) _____ extra points if you serve everybody correctly. Watch me and you'll understand. Oh, no! I've just dropped a pizza. I definitely (**6**) _____ a high score this time! Actually, I (**7**) _____ now because I'm a bit tired. I might play again tomorrow. Why not try it yourself? I'm sure you (**8**) _____ it!

**5** Complete the sentences. Use the second conditional form of the verbs in brackets.

1  If we _____ (have)
   £1 million, we _____
   (not know) what to do.
2  If you _____ (buy) a
   printer, you _____ (find)
   it really useful.
3  It _____ (be) strange
   if it _____ (snow) in
   Italy in summer.
4  I _____ (not like) it if
   I _____ (live) in a cold country.
5  If you _____ (meet) the
   Queen, what _____ (you /
   say)?

**6** Complete the sentences with the quantifiers in the box.

| any   a few   a little   a lot of   many   much |

1  He invited thirty friends to his party, but only
   _____ people came.
2  'Here are some crisps.'
   'Stop! I don't want too _____.'
3  Mary is very popular. She's got _____ of
   friends.
4  'Would you like some cake?'
   'Just _____. I'm not very hungry.'
5  We've eaten all the biscuits. There aren't
   _____ more in the cupboard.
6  I can't afford a new CD. I haven't got
   _____ money this month.

**7** Correct the mistake in each sentence.

1  As soon as it'll stop raining, we'll go out.
   _____
   _____
2  If I liked swimming, I'll go to the pool every day.
   _____
   _____
3  Look at the tickets! We've flying to London on
   Monday.
   _____
   _____
4  Here's some water. You won't be thirsty if you
   drank some.
   _____
   _____
5  Jake is shy so he's only got a little friends.
   _____
   _____
6  It'll be dark by the time the match finish.
   _____
   _____

**8** Complete the dialogue with the words in the box.

| a lot of   any   Are you doing   buy   decide   'll be
  many   'm meeting   're going to get   won't have |

Rob   (1) _____ anything on
      Saturday afternoon?
Lisa  Yes, I (2) _____ Sue
      in town. We (3) _____
      some new shoes.
Rob   Shoes? You don't need (4) _____
      more shoes!
Lisa  Yes, I do. I haven't got (5) _____
      pairs!
**In a shoe shop ...**
Sue   They're really cool.
Lisa  Yes, but they're very expensive.
      If I (6) _____ these,
      I (7) _____ much money left.
      Do you prefer the other ones?
Sue   Come on, Lisa! You've tried on
      (8) _____ shoes this afternoon.
      It (9) _____ dark by the time you
      (10) _____ which ones to buy!

# Culture focus

**1** Do the culture quiz. Look for the answers in your Student's Book and Workbook if necessary.

## Section A  Complete the crossword with the names of countries.
*(1 point for each correct answer)*

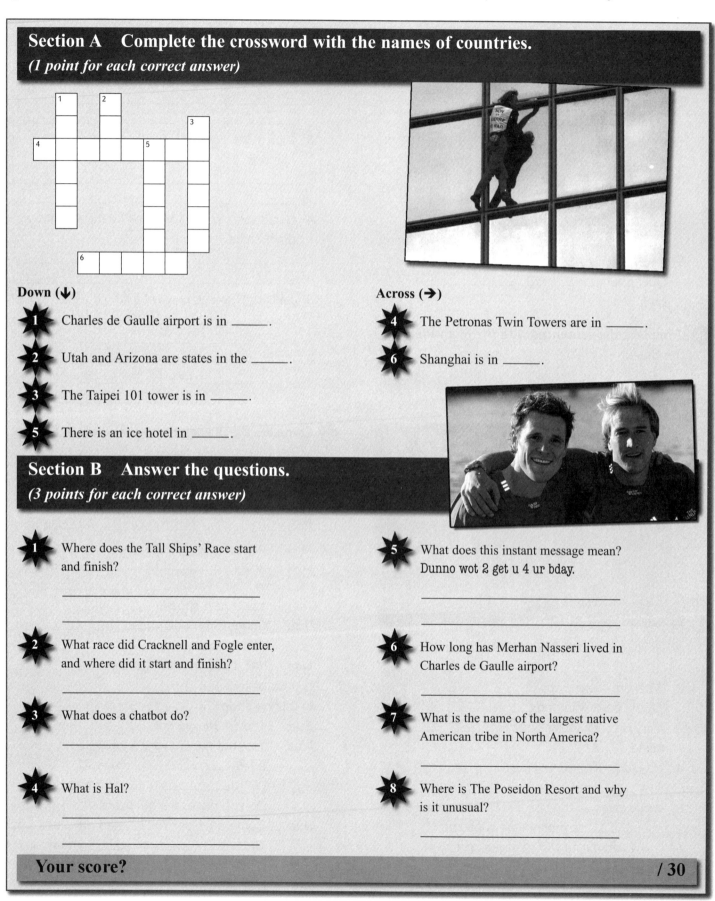

**Down (↓)**

**1** Charles de Gaulle airport is in _____.

**2** Utah and Arizona are states in the _____.

**3** The Taipei 101 tower is in _____.

**5** There is an ice hotel in _____.

**Across (→)**

**4** The Petronas Twin Towers are in _____.

**6** Shanghai is in _____.

## Section B  Answer the questions.
*(3 points for each correct answer)*

**1** Where does the Tall Ships' Race start and finish?

_____

_____

**2** What race did Cracknell and Fogle enter, and where did it start and finish?

_____

**3** What does a chatbot do?

_____

**4** What is Hal?

_____

_____

**5** What does this instant message mean?
Dunno wot 2 get u 4 ur bday.

_____

_____

**6** How long has Merhan Nasseri lived in Charles de Gaulle airport?

_____

**7** What is the name of the largest native American tribe in North America?

_____

**8** Where is The Poseidon Resort and why is it unusual?

_____

**Your score?** / 30

## Reading

# A head for heights

**A** Dan McCallum is a 21-year-old student from Sydney, Australia. It is early on Saturday morning, but he has already been at work for two hours. He is standing with ten people 120 metres above the ground. This is because Dan works part-time as a tour guide on Sydney Harbour Bridge.

**B** It opened in 1932, and since the 2000 Olympic Games, it has become the most famous bridge in the world. Throughout the Games, the five Olympic rings decorated the bridge. At the end of the Olympics, it was the focus of a sensational firework display.

**C** In 1998, a tour company started offering a 1,500 metre walk and climb over the arch. Participants have to wear special suits and trainers, and a safety cord. Anybody over the age of twelve can do the tour, but you must be fit – and very brave. Parts of the arch are incredibly steep and the bridge's highest point is 134 metres above the harbour.

**D** 'We can rest at the top,' explains Dan, 'and you can enjoy the spectacular views. I'll take a photo of all of you as well.' Dan has to do this because climbers must not take any possessions

onto the bridge. If they dropped anything, it could be dangerous for the traffic and public below.

**E** You can do a daytime, an evening or a night climb. 'The climbs are all unique,' says Dan, 'but, in my opinion, the evening climb is the most dramatic. It's amazing to see the colours change across the sky and the sun set over the city. It's an experience you'll never forget.'

**1** Read the text. Then match paragraphs A–E with topics 1–6. (There is one topic you do not need.)

1 ☐ Dan's point of view
2 ☐ Essential equipment
3 ☐A☐ Dan's personal details
4 ☐ Climate
5 ☐ Historical information
6 ☐ Prohibitions

**2** Answer the questions. Use full sentences.

How does Dan spend his time?
*He is a tour guide and a student.*

1 Why is Sydney Harbour Bridge so well-known?
_____

2 What do the bridge climbers wear?
_____
_____

3 Can anybody climb the bridge? Why? / Why not?
_____
_____

4 Why is it necessary for climbers to be confident?
_____
_____

5 Why can't climbers take photographs?
_____
_____

# Grammar

## Modal verbs
### Ability and permission: *can* and *could*

**1** Match questions 1–6 with the answers a–f. Then complete the sentences with *can*, *can't*, *could* or *couldn't*.

1 [c] *Can* Anna and Emma wear jeans to school?
2 [ ] _____ you ski?
3 [ ] _____ you swim when you were six?
4 [ ] _____ I open the window, please?
5 [ ] Listen! _____ anybody hear the referee?
6 [ ] _____ you email each other when you were younger?

a No, we _____. The fans are too noisy!
b Yes, I _____. I first went in a pool when I was three.
c Yes, they *can* wear whatever they like.
d No, we _____. We didn't have computers then.
e Of course you _____. It's really hot in here.
f No, I _____. I've never done any winter sports.

**2** Complete the sentences. Use the verbs in the box with *can*, *can't*, *could* or *couldn't*.

> cycle   drink   listen   ~~play~~   ride   start up
> understand

We *can't play* squash, but we love watching it.
1 I _____ milk when I was a child, but I hate it now.
2 We _____ to school until we were eleven, but now we _____ our bikes every day.
3 He didn't do his homework because he _____ the question.
4 My mum _____ our computer. She isn't at all practical!
5 My dad turned off the radio because I _____ to music while I'm studying.

## Obligation and necessity: *have to* and *must*

**3** Complete the job advert with the words in the box.

> doesn't have to   don't have to   have   has
> ~~must~~   must   mustn't

### www.campamerica.com

# WANTED

*Young people to work in a children's summer camp in America.*

Applicants *must* be aged 18–22, be outgoing and enthusiastic. You **(1)** _____ also enjoy being outdoors. You will work with children, so you **(2)** _____ be a smoker.
Everybody **(3)** _____ to have a driving licence as some driving will be necessary. You **(4)** _____ speak fluent English, but it is an advantage.
Interested? All you **(5)** _____ to do is log on to the Camp America website and complete an application form.
The application **(6)** _____ be online.
If you prefer, post your completed form to:
Don Hatten, Camp America, 497 18th Street, New York, NY 10017

**4** Complete the sentences. Use the correct form of (*not*) *have to* or *mustn't* with the verbs in brackets.

I *have to buy* (buy) a present for Lisa. It's her birthday tomorrow.
1 You _____ (touch) the cooker! It's hot.
2 I _____ (do) the cleaning because it's my birthday!
3 You _____ (make) too much noise after eleven o'clock.
4 _____ (you / get up) early every morning?
5 You _____ (have) a rest right now. You decide.
6 I _____ (forget) to hand in my homework tomorrow.

## Advice and suggestions: *should*

**5** Complete the sentences. Use *should* or *shouldn't* and the phrases in the box.

> become a doctor   go near them   join a youth club
> stay up so late   ~~tell the teacher~~
> turn up the volume   wear a warm coat

Somebody is bullying me at school.
You *should tell the teacher.*

1 Lara is shy and she hasn't got many friends.
She _____

2 I can never get up in the mornings.
You _____

3 It's particularly cold today.
You _____

4 My brother is really good at science.
He _____

5 Those dogs don't look very friendly.
We _____

6 I can't hear the music.
They _____

## Consolidation

**6** Correct the mistake in each sentence.

You should to go to the doctor's.
*You should go to the doctor's.*

1 You must smoke in here. It's prohibited.
_____
_____

2 Jim can't speak Japanese last year, but he can now.
_____
_____

3 Do we must switch off our mobiles in class?
_____
_____

4 We're late. We have hurry.
_____

5 It'll be OK. You should no worry.
_____

6 My friend don't have to wear a uniform at school.
_____
_____

**7** Rewrite the sentences with *can, can't, could, couldn't, should* and *shouldn't.*

Don't eat in that restaurant. It's horrible.
You *shouldn't eat in that restaurant.*

1 The school doesn't let us use MP3 players.
We _____

2 Why not look for the information online?
You _____

3 Is it OK if I watch TV now?
_____ I _____

4 We were too young to apply for the job.
We _____

5 It's a good idea to revise before a test.
You _____

6 They had permission to go on the excursion.
They _____

**8** Complete the dialogue with the words in the box.

> can help   can surf   ~~can't do~~   couldn't think
> don't have to go   have to be   have to hand
> mustn't be   should plan   shouldn't start

**Linda** What's the matter?
**Amy** I'm trying to write an essay, but
I *can't do* it. I'm really worried because
I (1) _____ in the
essay tomorrow.
**Linda** I (2) _____ home yet,
so I (3) _____ you.
**Amy** Thanks! I don't know where to start.
**Linda** Well, you (4) _____
writing immediately. First, you
(5) _____ the essay
carefully. If you need any information,
you (6) _____ the
internet. How long does the essay
(7) _____?
**Amy** Between 350–500 words, but it
(8) _____ any longer.
**Linda** OK. What's the title?
**Amy** It's 'Discuss the causes of climate change'.
**Linda** What?
**Amy** Now you know why I (9) _____
_____ of anything to write!

# Communication

## Vocabulary   At school

**1** Find the nouns in the wordsquare and complete the phrases.

| A | D | P | R | O | J | E | C | T | S | C | L | D |
|---|---|---|---|---|---|---|---|---|---|---|---|---|
| W | E | B | S | I | T | E | E | H | R | O | E | E |
| T | E | X | C | U | R | S | I | O | N | U | S | T |
| H | T | E | M | A | R | B | D | M | K | R | O | E |
| E | N | C | E | A | M | S | X | E | A | S | N | N |
| L | T | H | X | M | A | W | O | W | T | E | S | T |
| H | I | S | A | T | R | E | X | O | A | S | E | I |
| E | O | P | M | O | K | H | I | R | R | E | S | O |
| S | N | L | E | S | S | O | N | K | B | T | O | N |

research a project

1  fail an e_____
2  have an English l_____
3  go on an e_____
4  get good m_____
5  hand in h_____
6  visit a w_____
7  have d_____
8  revise for a t_____
9  do a c_____

**2** Complete the sentences with the words in the box.

> break   bully   classes   copy   course   pass   ~~test~~

Have you revised for the spelling test?

1  Can you do a _____ in website design at your school?
2  Stop it! You shouldn't _____ people.
3  We have a _____ after our second lesson in the morning.
4  Did Jenny _____ your homework?
5  I've revised a lot. I'm sure I'll _____ the exam.
6  We only have three _____ today.

## Adjective + preposition

**3** Match the adjectives in the box with the correct preposition.

> ~~bad~~   tired   brilliant   interested   involved   relaxed   scared   upset

**at**
bad at
(1) _____

**about**
(2) _____
(3) _____

**in**
(4) _____
(5) _____

**of**
(6) _____
(7) _____

**4** Complete the sentences with an adjective and preposition from exercise 3.

I'm tired of watching TV. Let's go out!

1  I'm _____ _____ water, so I never go swimming.
2  Liz is crying. She's _____ _____ failing her exams last week.
3  We love going to museums because we're _____ _____ history.
4  That's beautiful! You're _____ _____ playing the piano.

## Speaking   A simple solution

**5** Put the conversation in the correct order.

a  ☐ What difference does it make watching it at your house?
b  ☐ 1 How about going to see that new film at the cinema?
c  ☐ You know, you shouldn't be scared of horror films. They aren't real.
d  ☐ Then we can switch on the lights when you get scared!
e  ☐ I know they aren't real, but I can't help it!
f  ☐ No way! It's a horror film.
g  ☐ Well, perhaps we should watch it at my house on DVD.

# Writing

## An opinion essay  Giving opinions

**1** Complete the first three paragraphs of the essay with the words in the box.

> example  believe  Also  well  think that  too  opinion  ~~such~~  like

## Extra-curricular clubs and activities

There are a lot of extra-curricular clubs and activities at my school, such as computer clubs, music clubs and sports clubs. In my (1) _____, participating in them is a very good idea for three main reasons.

I (2) _____ that attending school should not just be an educational activity. It should be sociable, (3) _____. After-school clubs are fun, and you can make friends with pupils in other classes and other years as (4) _____.

I (5) _____ going to a computer club is important. For (6) _____, if you have not got a computer at home, you can learn really useful skills, (7) _____ preparing documents, doing research on the internet and even programming. (8) _____, you can play really cool games.

In my opinion, _____

_____

_____

_____

_____

_____

Barbara Smith
Manchester

**2** Write the final paragraph in the correct order. Use the sentences in the box.

> After all, if you do not try something, you will never know what it is like!
> For example, I am learning the saxophone now because I first played one at a music club and I really enjoyed it.
> In my opinion, music clubs are a great idea, too.
> People should not be scared of playing unusual instruments.
> At these clubs, you can try playing a lot of different instruments.

# Quick check

## Vocabulary

**1** Complete the sentences with the words in the box.

> copied  got  had  passes  to research  revised

1 Harry _____ the same mark as me because he _____ my homework.
2 I feel confident because I've _____ for the test.
3 It can take a long time _____ a project.
4 Have you ever _____ detention?
5 We'll be really pleased if Sara _____ her exams.

**2** Choose the correct answer.

1 Is he experienced **in** / **at** teaching?
2 Mr Brown is a great maths teacher. He's **bad** / **good** at explaining things.
3 You shouldn't be scared **in** / **of** the dark.
4 She stopped reading because she got bored **of** / **at** the story.
5 I'm not **interested** / **involved** in art, so I don't want study it.
6 Are you worried **at** / **about** bullying at school?

## Vocabulary review: Units 1–7

**3** Choose the correct answer.

1 It took a long time to **make** / **get** breakfast today.
2 Has Beckham made any **decisions** / **noise** about the future?
3 You shouldn't be **rude** / **polite** to your teacher.
4 If you visit the **monitor** / **website**, you'll find the information.
5 Can you **take off** / **turn off** the lights when you go out, please?
6 I'm **tired** / **jealous** of this programme. Let's turn over.
7 My sister wants to **play** / **do** gymnastics.
8 We're really looking **forward** / **up** to the weekend.

## Grammar

**4** Complete the sentences. Use the verbs in the box with *can*, *can't*, *could* or *couldn't*.

> carry on  have  leave  you / play  you / study  understand

1 _____ tennis when you were eight?
2 In the UK, you _____ school until you're sixteen.
3 _____ art at your school now?
4 I'm tired. I _____ revising.
5 My last job was easy. I _____ a break whenever I wanted.
6 He was speaking Chinese. We _____ _____ anything that he said.

**5** Complete the dialogue with the verbs in the box.

> don't have to  have to  must  mustn't  should

**Tim** Where do I (1) _____ type the website address?
**Sally** Well, you (2) _____ log on to the internet first. It's connecting now. You (3) _____ wait very long, normally.
**Tim** Oh, no! I'm late. I'll turn off the computer.
**Sally** Stop! You (4) _____ be so impatient! It's important to shut down the computer correctly. You (5) _____ do a basic computer course!

## Grammar review: Units 1–7

**6** Choose the correct answer.

My father has (1) **already** / **just** had an interview for a new job. If he (2) **'ll get** / **gets** it, we'll move to Paris. And if we go to Paris, I (3) **won't** / **wouldn't** be very happy! I'm (4) **a few** / **a little** shy and I don't want (5) **speak** / **to speak** French. I've studied French (6) **for** / **since** years, but I (7) **couldn't** / **can't** speak it very well. If I could choose, I (8) **'d** / **'ll** definitely stay in this country.

# 8 Out of this world

## Reading

### Rare red cat

( Home )   ( Magazine )   ( Documentaries )   ( Subscriptions )

Every year, scientists identify a few new types of bird, about a hundred new species of fish and thousands of new insects. However, it is extremely rare to discover a new mammal, that is, an animal which has babies instead of eggs. Then, in 2005, an automatic camera photographed an unusual new mammal which really excited biologists.

Exploring in Borneo

The camera took two photographs deep in the jungles of Borneo. The creature looks like a red cat, but it is bigger and has a long, thick tail. It has long teeth, so it is probably carnivorous.

Borneo is in the South China Sea, north of Australia, and large areas of it are completely covered in dense jungle and rainforest. Borneo is the third largest island in the world after Greenland and New Guinea.

Scientists now want to catch the animal and examine it. If it really is a new mammal, it will be the first discovery of a new carnivore on Borneo in more than a century. The island is already home to more than 210 types of mammal. Amazingly, 44 of these species of mammal do not exist anywhere else in the world, so Borneo is one of the most important areas for wildlife on Earth.

However, Indonesia owns half of Borneo and it wants to create more farms. A lot of animal experts are worried because the Indonesian government plans to destroy an area of rainforest half the size of Holland. If this happens, it will also destroy a huge amount of wildlife, as well as the lives of the native people on the island. Unfortunately, the new cat-like mammal could become extinct before scientists know exactly what it is.

**1** **Read the text quickly and choose the correct answer.**

Scientists discover approximately ⟨100⟩ / 1,000 types of fish every year.
1  Mammals produce **babies** / **eggs**.
2  The new mammal is **the same as** / **similar to** a cat.
3  Carnivores have **large** / **strong** teeth.
4  Borneo is **bigger** / **smaller** than Greenland.
5  Somebody discovered a new mammal on Borneo more than **100** / **210** years ago.

**2** **Answer the questions. Use full sentences.**

Why were scientists interested in the photos?
*Because it is very unusual to find new mammals.*

1  Who or what took the photos?
   _____

2  What is the countryside like on Borneo?
   _____
   _____

3  How many species of mammal live only on Borneo?
   _____

4  Which country wants to replace Borneo's forests, and with what?
   _____
   _____

5  Who or what will the destruction of the forests affect?
   _____
   _____

# Grammar

## Relative clauses

*who, which* and *that*

**1** Match 1–7 with a–g to make complete sentences.

1  d  Borneo is an island …
2  ☐  Is she the scientist …
3  ☐  These are the trainers …
4  ☐  He is the person …
5  ☐  Is that the river …
6  ☐  Have you got the book …
7  ☐  Biology is a subject …

a  which you swam in?
b  that I bought yesterday.
c  who I sit next to in class.
d  that is north of Australia.
e  which I'd like to study.
f  who discovered the new mammal?
g  which I want to read?

**2** Complete the sentences with *who* or *which*.

I've never met anyone *who* has climbed Mount Everest.

1  Did you see the wildlife programme _____ was on TV last night?
2  Mary is scared of animals _____ bite.
3  Have you heard about the couple _____ got married underwater?
4  I don't know anybody _____ plays rugby.
5  Ian told us a story _____ we didn't believe.
6  This is the CD _____ Mark gave me.
7  Jane is somebody _____ finds it hard to make friends.
8  There aren't many people _____ can run 100 metres in 12 seconds.

**3** Complete the text with the words in the box.

that includes   ~~that is~~   that live   that he thought   which have   which is   which translates   who gave   who go

# Quokkas

Home   Magazine   Documentaries   Subscriptions

Rottnest is a beautiful island *that is* near Perth, in Western Australia. It was a 17th century Dutch explorer, Willem de Vlamingh, (1) _____ the island its name. 'Rottenest' is a Dutch word (2) _____ as 'rat's nest' in English. This is because, while he was sailing past the island, Willem de Vlamingh saw a lot of animals (3) _____ were large rats. However, they weren't rats. They were, in fact, quokkas.

Quokkas are small mammals (4) _____ a rounded body, a short tail, and a wide, flat face. They look similar to a rat, but they are a 'marsupial'. Marsupial is the type of animal (5) _____ kangaroos.

Rottnest has a habitat (6) _____ ideal for these herbivores. There are probably about 10,000 quokkas (7) _____ on the island. As a result, tourists on Rottnest (8) _____ for a swim often find a quokka sitting on their towels when they get back!

## who or whose?

**4** Write sentences with *who* or *whose*.

I don't know / is singing / this song
*I don't know who is singing this song.*

1 does / anybody / know / money / this is / ?

_____

_____

2 she's / the new actress / films / I / love

_____

_____

3 I / wouldn't / marry / anybody / is famous

_____

_____

4 that's / the neighbour / children / are / really noisy

_____

_____

5 I've got / a friend / has touched / a quokka

_____

_____

6 do / you / know / anybody / can / tell / a good joke / ?

_____

_____

**5** Complete the sentences with *who*, *who's* or *whose*.

Lola is the person *who* emails me every week.
1 This is the girl _____ brother lives in Dubai.
2 Do you know anybody _____ run a marathon?
3 She's an author _____ books are really popular in the USA.
4 Columbus is the explorer _____ discovered America.
5 What's the name of the girl _____ wearing goggles?
6 We can't understand people _____ speak English really quickly.
7 The teacher asked us _____ mobile phone was ringing.
8 He's the boy _____ got short black hair.

## Consolidation

**6** Correct the mistake in each sentence.

That's the student which cheated in the test.
*That's the student who / that cheated in the test.*

1 The person whose talking now will have detention.

_____

_____

2 Where's the fish who James caught?

_____

3 We aren't sure who's lives here.

_____

4 Is this the film what he liked?

_____

5 Is she the girl which is interested in animals?

_____

_____

6 Where is the CD you which borrowed?

_____

_____

**7** Complete the text with relative pronouns.

### April Fools

I must tell you about something funny *which / that* happened at school. I've got a science teacher
(1) _____ lessons are usually very boring, but she was ill last week. Mr King is the teacher
(2) _____ taught us instead. At the end of his lesson, he showed us a picture of an unusual plant (3) _____ had long things on it
(4) _____ looked like spaghetti. Nobody knew its name, so we had to research it for homework.

I visited a website (5) _____ is usually very useful, but I couldn't find the answer. My grandmother is the sort of person (6) _____ knows everything, so I showed the picture to her. But even she couldn't help! By the next lesson, we still didn't know its name. Mr King was smiling as he wrote the date on the board, and we suddenly realised it was all a joke. It was Thursday, 1st April! The picture was of a plant (7) _____ doesn't exist.

# Communication

## Vocabulary   The natural world

**1** Complete the puzzle. What is the mystery natural world word?

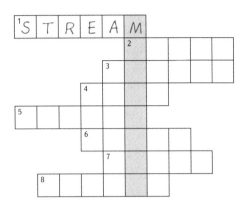

The mystery natural world word is _____ .

1   In summer, 7 can become a _____ .
2   The Atlantic is an _____ .
3   The trees and other plants on Borneo form
    a _____ .
4   You find _____ on 6.
5   There are a lot of trees in a _____ .
6   If you go to the _____ , you can go swimming.
7   The Nile is a _____ .
8   Bahrain is an _____ .

## Verb + preposition

**2** Complete the sentences with the correct verbs and prepositions.

> Would you like to listen to my MP3 player?

1   My parents sometimes a_____
    a_____ money.
2   'He isn't coming.' 'Let's w_____
    f_____ another five minutes!'
3   T_____ a_____ the title
    of the essay before you write it.
4   Brenda is insensitive. She doesn't
    c_____ a_____ other
    people's feelings.
5   Adam and Mark are really boring. They
    t_____ a_____ the same
    thing all the time.

**3** Match 1–7 with a–g to make complete sentences.

1   [e]   Did you listen ...
2   [ ]   Have you looked ...
3   [ ]   I'm sorry, but we asked ...
4   [ ]   Is James there? I need to talk ...
5   [ ]   I'm really worried ...
6   [ ]   Scientists are always looking ...
7   [ ]   Our school specialises ...

a   to him.
b   for new species of animal.
c   for coffee, not tea.
d   in languages.
e   to the radio last night?
f   about climate change.
g   at the information that I gave you?

## Speaking   A book review

**4** Complete the dialogue with the words in the box.

> bit  ~~book~~  characters  completely  couldn't
> ending  exciting  long  Really  shouldn't  way

**Fiona**  What did you think about the book, then?
**Shaun**  I quite enjoyed it, but it was very
          **(1)** _____ and I thought the
          **(2)** _____ was rubbish.
**Fiona**  I **(3)** _____ agree more. And the
          **(4)** _____ weren't very
          interesting, either.
**Shaun**  Yeah, but I loved it when she was waiting
          for him to come back. That was
          **(5)** _____ .
**Fiona**  I **(6)** _____ disagree! I thought
          that **(7)** _____ was really boring.
          They definitely **(8)** _____ make a
          film of it.
**Shaun**  **(9)** _____ ? Well, I think I'll read
          another book by the same author.
**Fiona**  No **(10)** _____ ! I'm going to try
          somebody different.

# Writing

## A description of a place

### Sentence adverbs

**1** Complete the text with the phrases in the box.

> clearly different from the Mediterranean    fortunately, it does not get too hot    honestly, it looks just
> luckily, they are not as crowded    obviously good news for the tourists    unfortunately for hoteliers
> unfortunately, an umbrella is as useful

When British people think of Spain, they usually think of sun, sea and sand. However, I have just visited Asturias, in the north-west of Spain, which is *clearly different from the Mediterranean.*

I was surprised at the scenery because it is so similar to where I live. (1) _____ like Scotland!

Asturias is quite rainy, even in summer. The rain makes the scenery really green and, (2) _____ _____, like the south of Spain.

(3) _____ as a swimming costume!

There are really beautiful beaches along the coast and (4) _____ as the Costa del Sol. (5) _____, the region is not particularly popular with foreign tourists yet, probably because of the weather. But this is (6) _____ _____ who do visit Asturias.

_____

_____

_____

Tim Curtis
Lemmington, Scotland

**2** Match 1–3 with a–c. Then complete the final paragraph of the text.

1 [c] When you leave the coast, …
2 [ ] There are a lot of forests and lakes …
3 [ ] People say that bears and wolves still live in the forests, …

a but unfortunately, I didn't see any!
b which are extremely beautiful.
c you can see the spectacular Cantabrian mountains.

**3** Read the text again. Then answer the questions with *Yes* or *No*.

1 Is Asturias famous for its sun, sea and sand?
   _____
2 Does the writer think that Asturias really looks like Scotland? _____
3 Does the writer enjoy hot summers? _____
4 Does the writer like busy beaches? _____
5 Does the writer think that Asturias is a good tourist destination? _____
6 Did the writer want to see some wild animals?
   _____

## Vocabulary

**1** **Choose the correct answer.**

Last summer holidays, we stayed on Skye, an
(1) **island / ocean** in Scotland. There was a small
(2) **river / stream** in the garden. We couldn't swim
because it wasn't as deep as a (3) **river / stream**, so
we threw (4) **rocks / sand** and stones into it instead!
There was a (5) **jungle / forest** near us, and some
amazing (6) **beaches / deserts** which were
completely empty.

**2** **Complete the sentences. Use the verbs in the box with *about*, *for* or *to*.**

| ask listen talk think wait worry |

1 Let's _____ the Radio 1 news.
  It's on now.
2 _____ your homework before
  you write it.
3 Did you _____ her on the
  phone?
4 We won't be long. _____ us!
5 Don't _____ me. I'll be fine.
6 I'm hungry. I'll _____ two
  burgers.

## Vocabulary review: Units 1–8

**3** **Complete the sentences with the verbs in the box.**

| argue carry give hand look plug revise turn |

1 Did you _____ in your homework
  on time?
2 I never _____ forward to exams!
3 Where can I _____ in my mobile?
4 'Let's stop!' 'No! Let's _____ on!'
5 Don't _____ up. You can win!
6 Please _____ on the lights! I'm scared
  of the dark.
7 Are you going to _____ for the test?
8 Harry is miserable. He always wants to
  _____ about everything!

## Grammar

**4** **Choose the correct relative pronoun.**

1 A chef is somebody **which / that** cooks food.
2 An MP3 player is a machine **which / who** plays
  music.
3 There are 44 mammals **that / who** only exist on
  Borneo.
4 New York is a city **which / who** I want to see.
5 We don't know anybody **which / that** can speak
  Chinese.
6 Is she the actress **which / who** you like?

**5** **Complete the sentences with *who*, *who's* or *whose*.**

1 It is Brian _____ a friend of Jake's.
2 We don't know _____ this bag is.
3 Emma is somebody _____ is very
  hard-working.
4 They're the people _____ play in our
  band.
5 Is that the man _____ run three
  marathons?
6 I'm the sort of person _____ cares
  about the environment.

## Grammar review: Units 1–8

**6** **Choose the correct answer.**

I (1) **'m doing / 've done** a science degree at
university at the moment. It's something I've
(2) **always / yet** wanted to do because I (3) **was /
been** very good at science at school. I'm really
excited because next month I (4) **'m travelling /
've travelled** to the island of Madagascar, in Africa.
I want (5) **to work / work** with some scientists there
for the summer. They are the people (6) **who / which**
discovered two new species of lemur on the island
last year. There are a lot of very rare animals on
Madagascar, so it (7) **won't / 'll** be an amazing place
to work. It would be incredible if I (8) **'d discover /
discovered** a new species while I was working there!

## Reading

# Don't drop it!

**A** People have chewed gum for thousands of years. Two thousand years ago, the ancient Greeks chewed 'mastiche', resin from the mastic tree. Later, in central America, the Mayans chewed 'chicle'. This comes from the sapodilla tree and was the main ingredient for chewing gum until the 1940s.

**B** In the UK, millions of people chew gum every day. Afterwards, some people throw it in a bin, but others just drop it on the ground. As a result, the streets are covered in millions of small white dots of dried chewing gum.

**C** It is difficult to remove dried chewing gum, and it costs £150 million a year to clean gum off the streets: that is about £3 per person per year! So, in some parts of the country, councils have decided to stop the problem. In Preston, the council has made special boards where people can stick their used gum. And if the police see you drop gum in the street, you will have to pay a £50–75 fine.

**D** In other areas, adverts in shopping centres remind people to throw their used gum in a bin. Some places even have special bags for people to put their gum into. Environmentalists want the price of gum to go up. Chewing gum manufacturers can then use the extra money to clean the streets.

**E** There are quite a lot of anti-chewing gum ideas in the UK – but nowhere is as radical as Singapore. The Singaporean government prohibited chewing gum in 1992 because of the problem of dirty streets. If you import gum into the country, you could go to prison or pay a $1,000 fine. Just imagine what would happen if you chewed it!

**1** Read the text. Then match paragraphs A–E with headings 1–6. (There is one heading you do not need.)

1 ☐ An expensive problem
2 ☐ The cost of advertising
3 ☐ Against the law
4 ☐ *A* An ancient habit
5 ☐ Anti-gum ideas
6 ☐ Dirty habits

**2** Answer the questions. Use full sentences.

Who invented chewing gum and when?
*The Greeks made chewing gum from the mastic tree two thousand years ago.*

1 What problem does gum cause? How?

_____

_____

2 How do they stop people dropping gum in Preston?

_____

_____

3 Why do some environmentalists want people to pay more for gum?

_____

_____

4 Which is the worst place in the world to chew gum? Why?

_____

_____

# Grammar

## The passive

**1** **Complete the interview with the words in the box.**

> are downloaded   aren't needed   aren't given
> are new songs played   is played   is copied
> is created   isn't downloaded   ~~isn't sold~~   are sold

**Mr Olds** We've just listened to a new single on the radio, but it *isn't sold* in the shops yet. Why **(1)** _____ _____ on the radio before they are released to the public?

**DJ Dodgy** Basically, it's for marketing. A new song **(2)** _____ on the radio or advertised on TV before it is released to the public. That's how interest in the song **(3)** _____ before people can actually buy it. Then, thousands of copies of a song **(4)** _____ as soon as it appears in the shops.

**Mr Olds** Now, the music I listen to **(5)** _____ _____ from the internet, but these days billions of songs **(6)** _____ onto computers. Does this mean that CDs **(7)** _____ any more?

**DJ Dodgy** No, it doesn't. Although the amount of music which **(8)** _____ from the internet has increased enormously over the past year, CDs will always have a future. For example, music downloads **(9)** _____ as presents, so CDs are still popular for birthdays.

**2** **Write sentences in the present simple passive.**

my father / employ / by the government
*My father is employed by the government.*

1  millions of computers / make / in Asia
_____

2  cars / not produce / here any more
_____

3  a lot of money / spend / on education
_____

4  he / teach / by a professional / ?
_____

5  I / not pay / much
_____

6  these adverts / see / by many people / ?
_____

**3** **Complete the sentences. Use the present simple passive form of the verbs in the box.**

> these T-shirts / make   ~~celebrate~~   export
> not use   not wear   this book / published   visit

The new year *is celebrated* on 1 January.

1  That website _____ by hundreds of people every day.

2  Because of the internet, book encyclopedias _____ as much.

3  A lot of Greek olive oil _____ to the UK.

4  _____ by Oxford University Press?

5  Jeans _____ at our school.

6  _____ in China?

**4** Write the stages of producing an album in the correct order. Use the present simple passive.

> the CDs / distribute / to shops
> the CDs / produce       the songs / rehearse
> the music / compose     ~~the lyrics / write~~
> the album / record / in a studio
> the songs / play / on the radio

The lyrics are written.

1 _____
2 _____
3 _____
4 _____
5 _____
6 _____

**5** Complete the sentences with the correct active or passive form of the verbs.

> They sell home-made soup in that shop.
> Home-made soup is sold in that shop.

1 People play baseball in America.
  Baseball _____ in America.
2 Typewriters aren't used these days.
  People _____ typewriters these days.
3 In hotels, somebody makes your bed.
  In hotels, your bed _____ .
4 My brother designs those computer games.
  Those computer games _____
  by my brother.
5 Beckham is paid thousands of dollars a week.
  Beckham's club _____ him thousands
  of dollars a week.
6 Oranges aren't grown in England.
  They _____ oranges in England.

**6** Rewrite the active sentences in the passive. Only include information about who does the action if it is necessary.

> My parents own this restaurant.
> This restaurant is owned by my parents.

1 Scientists discover new insects every year.
  _____
  _____
2 They don't sell computers here.
  _____
  _____
3 They sing most of their songs in English.
  _____
  _____
4 People don't import petrol into Saudi Arabia.
  _____
  _____
5 They show the World Cup on TV all over the world.
  _____
  _____
6 They play tennis at Wimbledon in June.
  _____
  _____

## Consolidation

**7** Complete the text with the active or passive form of the verbs in brackets.

Are we influenced (we / influence) by the advertising which _____ (**1** appear) on sportspeople's shirts? For example, the names of mobile phone companies _____ (**2** write) on a lot of footballers' shirts. _____ (**3** certain mobiles / choose) just because of the adverts? Some people say, 'No.' They _____ (**4** insist) that their decisions _____ (**5** not affect) by sports advertising. However, mobile phone companies _____ (**6** believe) that we really _____ (**7** influence) by advertising. As a result, an enormous amount of money _____ (**8** spend) so that advertisers _____ (**9** connect) to the best football clubs in the country.

# Communication

## Vocabulary  Money

**1**  Complete the crossword.

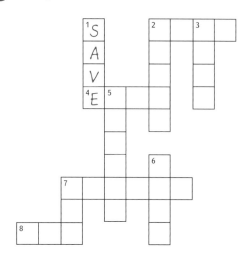

### Down (↓)

1  You should _____ a little money every month.
2  I _____ £4.50 every month at the cinema.
3  I haven't got any money. Can you _____ me £20?
5  That's too expensive. We can't _____ it.
6  How much does that MP3 player _____ ?
7  I need to _____ a present for Jane.

### Across (→)

2  Do they _____ chewing gum in the newsagent's?
4  If he does that job, he'll _____ £1,000 a month.
7  Can I _____ £2? I'll give it back tomorrow.
8  You should _____ about £1.50 for two tickets.

## -ed and -ing adjectives

**2**  Complete the pairs of sentences. Use the *-ed* and *-ing* adjective forms of the verbs in the box.

| amaze   frighten   interest   tire |

1a  If you're *tired*, you should have a break.
 b  Running a marathon is extremely _____ .
2a  Is Carla _____ of spiders?
 b  Horror films are very _____ .
3a  Are you _____ in selling your printer?
 b  I visited a really _____ website last night.
4a  My teacher was _____ that I passed all my exams.
 b  That was _____ ! I want to do it again.

## Speaking  Can you guess?

**3**  Complete the dialogue with the phrases in the box.

| Are there  Are they  Is it  it is  it isn't  made in made of  ~~that is~~  there are  they are |

**Ann**  I'm thinking of something *that is* in my school bag.
**Sue**  Is it (1) _____ Europe?
**Ann**  Yes, (2) _____ .
**Sue**  Is it (3) _____ plastic?
**Ann**  No, (4) _____ .
**Sue**  (5) _____ a few in your bag?
**Ann**  Yes, (6) _____ .
**Sue**  (7) _____ made of wood?
**Ann**  Yes, (8) _____ .
**Sue**  (9) _____ a pencil?
**Ann**  Yes, it is!

# Writing

## A discussion essay   Writing review

**1** Complete the essay with the phrases in the box.

Also  but  extremely  Finally  for example  I believe  my opinion
I think  not at all  one hand  other hand  so  such as

### The internet

These days, the internet is used all the time. I *believe* that the internet is really useful,
**(1)** _____ there are pros and cons which we should consider.

On the **(2)** _____, the internet is a very fast way to find out information. It is also very
easy to use, **(3)** _____ people who are inexperienced can surf the net quite easily.

Additionally, a lot of goods are bought and sold on the internet. This is **(4)** _____ helpful
for people who cannot get to the shops. Products **(5)** _____ books and CDs are often
cheaper on the internet, too.

Another advantage is that people can communicate with each other online, **(6)** _____, by
instant messaging or emailing. **(7)** _____ that this is great, especially if your family or
friends live in a different town or country.

On the **(8)** _____, there are some disadvantages to the internet. First of all, if you want
the internet at home, it will cost a lot to buy a computer.

Secondly, too much homework is researched on the internet. It is **(9)** _____ fair if you
have not got a computer at home. **(10)** _____, it is a pity that people do not look at books
and encyclopedias as much.

**(11)** _____, in **(12)** _____, communicating by email is impersonal. People often
use email to avoid speaking to somebody, especially if they have something difficult to say.

**2** Put the words of the final paragraph in the correct order.

1  believe / that / is / I / really / the internet / technology. / amazing
2  it / everything. / use / we / not / However, / for / should
3  presume / should / Also, / is / we / that / not / connected. / everybody

I believe _____

_____

_____

_____

# Quick check

## Vocabulary

**1** Complete the text with the money verbs in the box.

> afford   buy   cost   save   sell   spend

It's often cheaper to (1) _____ things online than in the shops. If you look carefully, you'll (2) _____ a lot of money. For example, the new computer game which I wanted was really expensive in the shops and I definitely couldn't (3) _____ it. However, when I surfed the net, the game (4) _____ much less online. Also, some people (5) _____ second-hand games online when they've finished with them. It's a good idea to get second-hand games if you haven't got much money to (6) _____ .

**2** Complete the sentences with the *-ed* or *-ing* adjective form of the verbs in brackets.

1 Everybody was _____ (shock) when they heard the news.
2 Travelling can be very _____ (tire).
3 This is _____ (bore)! I'm going to turn over.
4 I'm not _____ (interest) in politics.
5 Don't read that book! It's _____ (terrify).
6 We were _____ (amaze) when we saw the film.

## Vocabulary review: Units 1–9

**3** Choose the correct answer.

1 If you're **worried / relaxed** about something, talk to Jenny. She's kind and **insensitive / sensitive**.
2 It's **honest / dishonest** to **cheat / bully** in an exam.
3 The view from the top of the **mountain / island** was **amazed / amazing**.
4 Can I **borrow / lend** your dictionary? I want to look **into / up** a word.
5 She is jealous **about / of** you because you're **going / getting** married.
6 Peter is so **lazy / hard-working**. He never **makes / does** an effort.

## Grammar

**4** Complete the sentences with the passive form of the verbs in the box.

> not make   she / pay   sell   send
> you / teach   use

1 Those shoes _____ of leather.
2 The cheapest computers _____ on that website.
3 _____ £4 an hour for working in the café?
4 _____ computer programming at school?
5 Adverts _____ to sell products.
6 Serious criminals _____ to prison.

**5** Choose the correct answer.

1 Our decisions **influence / are influenced** by adverts.
2 A lot of young people **involve / are involved** in the campaign.
3 Digital cameras **cost / are cost** a lot of money.
4 Cheese **produces / is produced** in my village.
5 That restaurant **makes / is made** amazing food.
6 Classical music **doesn't play / isn't played** much on the radio.

## Grammar review: Units 1–9

**6** Complete the text with the correct form of the verbs in brackets.

I _____ (1 just / see) an advert in the window of a new café in the centre of town. The café _____ (2 call) Purple and they need people to dye their hair purple _____ (3 advertise) the café – and you _____ (4 pay) £100 for doing it. I want _____ (5 buy) a digital camera but I _____ (6 not save) enough money yet. I'm interested, as I'd get £100 if I _____ (7 do) it. However, if I changed the colour of my hair, my head teacher _____ (8 not like) it: purple hair _____ (9 not allow) at my school!

# Revision: Units 7-9

**1** **Complete the advert with the words in the box.**

> afford   scared   amazed   amazing   interested   involved   island   jungle   saved   website

## Animal Asia

Are you (1) _____ in animals? So, you'd like to see the hundreds of unusual animals which live in the (2) _____? Well, why not visit the (3) _____ of Borneo?

It doesn't matter if you're (4) _____ of flying or if you haven't (5) _____ enough money to fly to Borneo! Anybody can (6) _____ an excursion to *AnimalAsia* – because it's **FREE**!

*AnimalAsia* is the (7) _____ new exhibition at the Science Museum next month. Come and look at the animals in their natural habitat – you can even get (8) _____ in feeding some of them.

For more information, visit our (9) _____. And prepare to be (10) _____!

**2** **Complete the sentences. Use the *-ed* or *-ing* adjective form of the verbs in the box.**

> bore   interest   relax   surprise   terrify   worry

1 We heard a _____ noise while we were walking home last night. It sounded like a lion!
2 Are you _____ about the exams in May? I'm really nervous!
3 Do you ever get _____ of revising?
4 The sound of the sea was so _____, I fell asleep on the beach.
5 It's _____ that James failed the test. We thought he would pass.
6 I love history. It's so _____.

**3** **Complete the sentences with the correct preposition.**

1 How long will it take to revise _____ the test?
2 Why is your sister jealous _____ you?
3 Did you argue _____ money?
4 I didn't ask _____ any help.
5 Sally is selfish. She doesn't care _____ anybody except herself.
6 Nick won't listen _____ me when he's angry.
7 We should think _____ our science project.
8 Look _____ that amazing animal over there!
9 What is your sister specialising _____ at university?
10 Wait _____ us!

# Grammar

**1** Complete the dialogue with the modal verbs in the box.

> can   can't   couldn't   mustn't   should
> shouldn't

**Teacher**  You look terrible.

**Sid**  Yes, miss. I **(1)** _____ sleep last night and now I **(2)** _____ concentrate because I'm so tired.

**Teacher**  Really? You **(3)** _____ go home and go back to bed. You definitely **(4)** _____ stay at school.

**Sid**  But what about the lesson?

**Teacher**  You **(5)** _____ worry about that now. You **(6)** _____ copy anything that is important from me.

**2** Choose the correct modal verbs. Then answer question 8.

> You **(1) have / must** to be confident because you appear on TV.
>
> You **(2) should / could** always be well-dressed.
>
> You **(3) have to / don't have to** speak clearly so that everybody **(4) could / can** understand you.
>
> You **(5) couldn't / mustn't** speak too quickly.
>
> You **(6) should / shouldn't** do this job if you are interested in the weather.
>
> Some people who do this job work at weekends, but I **(7) mustn't / don't have to**.
>
> What is my job? **(8)** _____

**3** Complete the sentences with *who / that*, *which / that* or *whose*.

1  Have you seen any shoes _____ you like?
2  I've never met anybody _____ is famous.
3  Tony is talking to some friends _____ live in France.
4  She's lost an MP3 player _____ cost a lot of money.
5  Is that your friend _____ sister appears on TV?
6  A tour guide is a job _____ can be really interesting.
7  Chelsea FC has a manager _____ is Portuguese.
8  I can never remember _____ handwriting this is.

**4** Rewrite the active sentences in the passive. Only include information about who does the action if it is necessary.

1  People spend a lot of money on fashion.
_____
_____

2  They grow tea in China.
_____
_____

3  Millions of people watch football matches every weekend.
_____
_____

4  Schools in the UK teach French.
_____
_____

5  They don't sell cheap trainers in that shop.
_____
_____

6  Do they make BMWs in Asia?
_____
_____

7  They don't play basketball at all UK schools.
_____
_____

8  Do you speak English here?
_____
_____

**5** Complete the sentences. Use the present simple active or passive form of the verbs in the box.

> drink   we / get   listen   play   teach   use
> visit   not wear

1  How many people _____ to that radio programme?
2  Millions of tourists _____ Egypt every year.
3  Mariam _____ English by a native speaker.
4  Tennis _____ on a court.
5  We _____ clothes like that any more.
6  How many cups of tea _____ every morning in the UK?
7  Rackets _____ for playing tennis.
8  Which day _____ the exam results?

**6** Correct the mistake in each sentence.

1  Have you seen the new boy whose started at our school?

_____

_____

2  Cheeses aren't produced in that region.

_____

3  I can play the piano now, but I can't when I was younger.

_____

_____

4  It's extremely hot, so you must eat it yet!

_____

_____

5  They've got a cousin which is really friendly.

_____

_____

6  Newspapers sell here.

_____

**7** Complete the text with the words in the box.

> can   couldn't   doesn't have to   has to
> have to   is imported   mustn't   should
> shouldn't   's made   which   who

## Poor Ollie!

My brother, Ollie, is feeling really miserable. He's hurt his leg, so he (1) _____ stay at home and rest. The doctor has given him a lot of orders. He (2) _____ walk on the leg for a few days (that's very important!) and he (3) _____ do any sport for a month, but he (4) _____ go swimming quite soon.

It all happened last Saturday. Ollie knows a boy (5) _____ has got an amazing skateboard. It's one (6) _____ is really fast because it (7) _____ of extremely light material, you know, an expensive one which (8) _____ from America. Anyway, Ollie borrowed the skateboard, but he (9) _____ stop and he crashed into a tree!

Personally, I don't think he (10) _____ worry about anything. You see, we (11) _____ do tests during the last week of term. Ollie can't go to school, so he (12) _____ do the tests. Lucky him!

# Culture focus

**1** Do the culture quiz. Look for the answers in your Student's Book and Workbook if necessary.

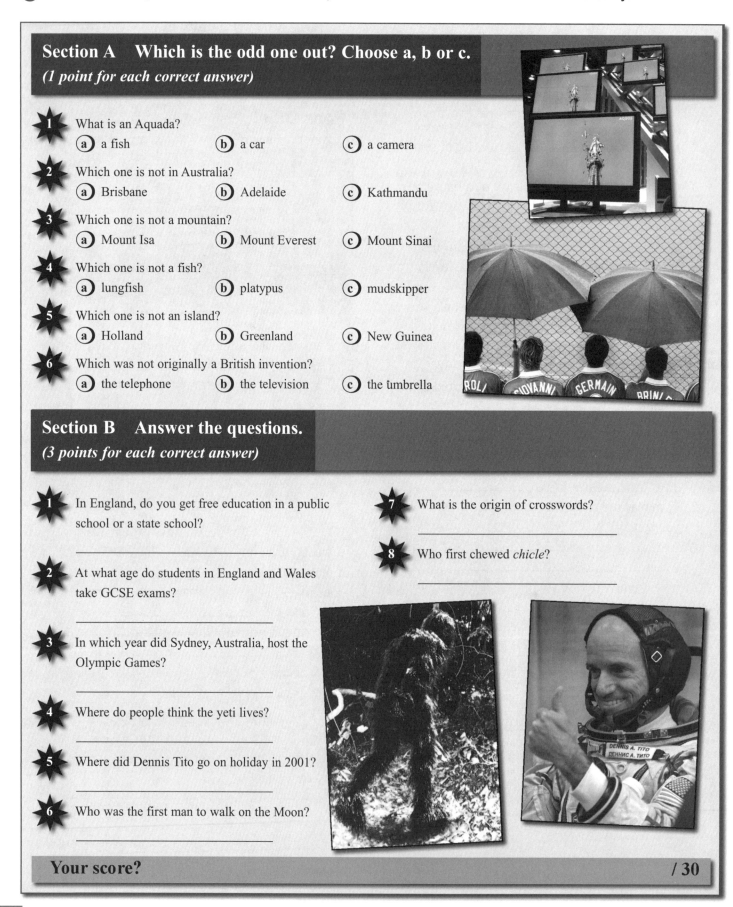

## Section A  Which is the odd one out? Choose a, b or c.
*(1 point for each correct answer)*

**1** What is an Aquada?
- **a** a fish
- **b** a car
- **c** a camera

**2** Which one is not in Australia?
- **a** Brisbane
- **b** Adelaide
- **c** Kathmandu

**3** Which one is not a mountain?
- **a** Mount Isa
- **b** Mount Everest
- **c** Mount Sinai

**4** Which one is not a fish?
- **a** lungfish
- **b** platypus
- **c** mudskipper

**5** Which one is not an island?
- **a** Holland
- **b** Greenland
- **c** New Guinea

**6** Which was not originally a British invention?
- **a** the telephone
- **b** the television
- **c** the umbrella

## Section B  Answer the questions.
*(3 points for each correct answer)*

**1** In England, do you get free education in a public school or a state school?

_____

**2** At what age do students in England and Wales take GCSE exams?

_____

**3** In which year did Sydney, Australia, host the Olympic Games?

_____

**4** Where do people think the yeti lives?

_____

**5** Where did Dennis Tito go on holiday in 2001?

_____

**6** Who was the first man to walk on the Moon?

_____

**7** What is the origin of crosswords?

_____

**8** Who first chewed *chicle*?

_____

**Your score?**                                                    **/ 30**